# LAUGHING AND LEARNING

## An Alternative to Shut Up and Listen

### Peter M. Jonas

ROWMAN & LITTLEFIELD EDUCATION
A division of
Rowman & Littlefield Publishers, Inc.
Lanham • New York • Toronto • Plymouth, UK

Published by Rowman & Littlefield Education
A division of Rowman & Littlefield Publishers, Inc.
A wholly owned subsidiary of The Rowman & Littlefield Publishing Group, Inc.
4501 Forbes Boulevard, Suite 200, Lanham, Maryland 20706
http://www.rowmaneducation.com

Estover Road, Plymouth PL6 7PY, United Kingdom

British Library Cataloguing in Publication Information Available

**Library of Congress Cataloging-in-Publication Data**
Jonas, Peter M.
  Laughing and learning : an alternative to shut up and listen / Peter M. Jonas.
    p. cm.
  Includes bibliographical references.
  ISBN 978-1-60709-316-9 (cloth : alk. paper) — ISBN 978-1-60709-317-6 (pbk. : alk. paper) — ISBN 978-1-60709-318-3 (electronic)
  1. Teaching. 2. Classroom environment. 3. Wit and humor in education. 4. Motivation in education. I. Title.
  LB1027.J58 2010
  371.102—dc22

                                                    2009027292

∞™ The paper used in this publication meets the minimum requirements of American National Standard for Information Sciences—Permanence of Paper for Printed Library Materials, ANSI/NISO Z39.48-1992.

Printed in the United States of America

Dedicated to Katie, Mel, and Kevin:
always learn, laugh, and live.

# CONTENTS

# FIGURES AND TABLES

# FOREWORD

*Robert J. Marzano*

For decades I have combed through the research and theory on instructional strategies that can enhance student achievement. While the use of humor comes up frequently as a potentially powerful instructional tool, I have never found a comprehensive, research-based treatment of the topic that speaks to the classroom teacher—until now.

It is certainly true that there are a number of books on humor, but the vast majority focus on how to write or tell jokes, or how to use humor in speeches, or they may simply be books explaining various aspects of humor, for example, joke books. Drawing on research and brain-based concepts, this book is unique because it presents a theoretical model, along with practical examples of its integration into the classroom and schools. The purpose of the book is to provide to teachers and administrators a research-based approach for using humor in schools. It is an attempt to explain eight strategies for using humor and then provide a variety of techniques that are designed to be practical applications. The intent is that teachers will be able to take the lessons learned and apply their own personal touch to improve the academic environment. One of the best aspects of the material is that you do not have to be a stand-up comic in order to use the information. In fact, the book is designed to apply to both the novice and master teacher. Peter Jonas provides an arsenal of tools that may be used in a variety of ways, depending on the subject matter, grades being taught, and one's own teaching style. There are not only action steps detailed on how to implement the strategies, but also specific guidelines listed in the book.

One strength, and unique character, of this book is that the ideas are not only practical but also supported by research. In addition to containing an extensive literature review, the material is the result of decades of structured observations and data collected from interviews, facilitation of workshops, and presentations conducted by the author throughout the country. While there are numerous jokes, stories, and funny exercises for everyone, additional sources, including specific websites, are identified for the reader to pursue.

Peter Jonas is able to identify eight different strategies for integrating humor into the learning environment through his research. Each of the eight strategies comprises a chapter, which starts with an overview of the research supporting the strategy, followed by action steps for implementing the strategy, and then practical examples, that is, jokes, stories, puns, and supporting humorous activities. The book is designed to be a practical guide (supported by research) to demonstrate that humor is a natural and fundamental activity that teachers and administrators need to utilize properly in order to enhance their effectiveness.

## OUTLINE OF BOOK

We read a lot about how difficult it is to develop a professional learning community and that it takes years to redirect the culture of any organization. However, Jonas explains in chapter 2 that using humor can improve the culture of a school in a shorter amount of time, with educators and students having fun at the same time. Chapter 3 may be the most interesting section of the book for teachers because it covers how to use humor to improve instruction. As the author notes, the key is to look spontaneous but to be very prepared. When used properly, humor helps students not only to remember information more effectively, but also to remember it longer—which is what learning is all about. Chapter 4 actually connects the previous two chapters by examining how humor builds relationships between teachers, students, and administrators, while enhancing the effectiveness of teamwork. For example, Provine (2000) explains that contrary to popular opinion, laughter is typically not a response to jokes, but is more of a human social signal solidifying relationships between individuals—pulling people together.

It is widely known, and accepted, that one basic element of successful leaders and teachers is good communication. Jonas covers this topic in chapter 5 by providing a rich theory and practical examples of using humor to improve communication from a multiplicity of angles. Moreover, as noted previously, the academic environment is becoming more complex and stressful. Chapter 6 investigates the effect humor has on reducing stress and tension for people in a variety of situations. Jonas notes that there are both physical and psychological benefits of humor. For example, research from the University of Maryland Medical Center in Baltimore indicates that laughter, and/or a sense of humor, can help protect people against a heart attack.

One of the things that may separate the "good" from the "great" teachers is creativity. Chapter 7 explains that there is a direct correlation between creativity and a sense of humor. Teachers who promote humor in class are able to help students become better critical thinkers while encouraging ingenuity.

In an interesting twist on research, chapter 8 investigates the effects of humor on promoting more positive student behavior in school. Specifically, humor promotes increased engagement by students; consequently, if students are paying more attention to the academic lessons, they are spending less time misbehaving. In addition, humor has been found to provide a means of social control because it can function as a mechanism to express approval or disapproval for the actions of students. The same may be said about group work. Humor can be used to promote teamwork and keep participants in line with the social norms.

Almost every school is challenged with the recruitment and retention of quality administrators and teachers. Chapter 9 covers this topic by demonstrating how humor allows teachers more freedom of expression and creativity, piquing their interest and joy in teaching. In other words, if administrators promote humor, teachers accept the challenge and thrive on the opportunity to try new techniques in class, thereby improving their interest in staying in the school district.

The final chapter of the book synthesizes all the research in a compact and usable fashion. Jonas provides guidelines for using humor in schools, warnings of what not to do, and discussions of topics not to cover and things teachers should avoid when telling jokes, for example, the use of sarcastic and demeaning humor. Ultimately, Jonas details ten main rules for properly integrating humor, rules that should help even the novice to be funny and successful.

One of the most interesting aspects of the book is the concept of *videagogy*—a term coined by the author. As most educators know, the term *pedagogy* is defined as the art, science, or profession of teaching. While researchers have identified numerous teaching styles that have proven to be successful, Jonas introduces the concept of using short, funny, digital videos in class to enhance teaching. Consequently, this new pedagogy, coupled with the use of videos, has been dubbed *videagogy*. I think the author has found something here. Teaching with short videos is not only a fun way to integrate humor but also a great way to utilize technology that matches the learning style of many young students entering our classrooms today.

Dale Carnegie wrote that "people rarely succeed unless they have fun in what they are doing." This book is a great example of how learning does not have to be a chore for teachers or students, but can be fun and engaging. It just takes a little practice, but the rewards are worth the efforts. Remember, you did not learn how to drive a car the first time you got behind the wheel. The same is true for integrating humor into teaching. In this book Peter Jonas has provided all classroom educators with powerful new instructional strategies that can be used in a variety of situations.

# ACKNOWLEDGMENTS

There is a local bicycle business that has a slogan: "Life is short, enjoy the ride." One way to enjoy the ride is to interject humor in all that you do. There is nothing like sharing a laugh to help relieve stress, make friends, and build relationships.

I grew up in a family that appreciated humor (thanks to my mother and father), so it was only natural to find a place to work that held the same high regard for humor. Humor is both encouraged and shared in my biological family, as well as with my "family" of friends and colleagues at Cardinal Stritch University, College of Education and Leadership. We truly have a culture of support, cooperation, and, most importantly, fun; this culture enhances the atmosphere of creativity, dedication, the pursuit of knowledge, and the capacity to learn. A culture of working hard and playing hard carries over to our doctoral students, many of whom suffer through all those long weekends of my courses that teach research, technology, and statistics, with a little humor thrown in. I owe a debt of gratitude to all the students. I also need to recognize the faculty in the doctoral leadership department, especially Dr. Mike Dickmann for all the jokes, cartoons, and videos—I may even reference some of the better ones. Thanks to my graduate students, Nick Constancio, Jessie Hegg, and Vince Kalt, for doing much of the "dirty work" on the research. And of course, no successful academic chairperson is worth anything without a great assistant, Denise Barnes. I also owe an intellectual debt to my family: Mel contributed a great deal by editing the book and having the creativity to envision the title—so if you do not like it, it is her fault; Katie provided practical information; Kevin was brutally honest about the humor; Andre provided moral support; and Elyse always smiled. An author always has to thank his wife—at least if he wants to stay married. Last but not least, I also want to give a shout-out to all the guys I play racquetball with—you put up with my jokes and sometimes you even provided me with some usable material.

# 1

# LAUGHING AND LEARNING, NOT LAUGHING *OR* LEARNING

**T**wo Martians found their way to Earth in order to learn all they could about the educational system in the United States. They gave a report to their leader that a school appears to be where the relatively young go to watch the relatively old work.

The only person who likes change is a baby with a wet diaper. Nevertheless, change is necessary in our educational system. There is a new and different generation in the classrooms today, technology has taken on its own life in education, and schools need to address the new knowledge, skills, and dispositions necessary for the twenty-first century. It seems as though educators tend to fall in love with the flavor of the day to revise our education system, for example, differentiated instruction, theory of multiple intelligence, brain-based research, writing across the curriculum, comprehensive school reform, strategic planning, and so forth. This book promotes a basic, simple, and natural concept: using humor to improve the learning environment.

## MYTHS ABOUT HUMOR

Let's start out with a few myths and facts about using humor in education. Myth number 1 is that everyone who writes about humor assumes that it is not a well-researched topic. This is incorrect. There have been numerous quality studies completed over the years on the topic. I am sure you know that to steal ideas from one person is plagiarism; to steal from many is research. Myth number 2 is that humor is not accepted into the mainstream of educators or researchers. This may be partially true, but a plethora of research studies has found that humor is a primary characteristic of successful teachers. Myth number 3 is that the process of humor needs to be dissected and analyzed to find the root cause. Definitely not true. E. B. White said, "Humor can be dissected as a frog, but the thing dies in the process." All researchers know about the superiority theory, incongruity theory, and relief theory of humor. Remember, all theories are wrong, but some are useful. However, the key to humor is to know when it works and how it can enhance the learning environment.

## FACTS ABOUT USING HUMOR

Here are some facts about humor that have been established through research:

1. Speakers are 46 percent more likely to laugh than listeners at their own jokes.
2. Many speakers even laugh at things that are typically not funny.
3. You're thirty times more likely to laugh when you're with other people than when you're alone.
4. Women laugh more than men.
5. Laughing is a social function. People will laugh at things not funny, if they are in groups. Laughter is not about humor, or jokes, but our social interactions (Provine, 2000, p. 47).
6. Male instructors can use almost all types of humor to increase their evaluation ratings.
7. Female instructors should avoid the use of puns or they are likely to greatly decrease their effectiveness ratings. (A jumper cable walks into a bar. The bartender says, "I'll serve you, but don't start anything.")

8. To be perceived as effective by students, instructors should use humor that adds to the content of education and contributes to the point (Edwards and Gibboney, 1992, pp. 22–23).
9. Men enjoy sexist, sexual, and aggressive humor more than women do, but women enjoy absurdity more than men do (Chapman and Gadfield, 1976).
10. Although women enjoy self-disparaging humor more, men apparently enjoy a speaker who disparages an enemy (Brooks, 1992).
11. Males use an average of 3.73 humorous items per class period, while females use only 2.43 items (Bryant, Comisky, and Zillmann, 1979). (Be careful with averages. I am sure you heard the story of a man who drowned crossing a stream with an average depth of six inches. ~ W. I. E. Gates.)
12. The most used format for humor is telling funny stories. Overall, the frequency and use of humor correlates positively to perceived appeal, effectiveness, and delivery for instructors, but for male instructors only.
13. Use of hostile or nonsense humor by male instructors is associated with higher overall performance evaluations, while the use of sexual humor is associated with greater appeal (Bryant, Comisky, and Zillmann, 1979).

However, remember that statistics like the ones cited above are not easy to understand; sometimes you have to go ANOVA and ANOVA a topic many times.

Here are the two main points of research: If you get people laughing you can tell them almost anything, and they will remember it longer and more efficiently. Instructors who use humor, even if it is not the best humor in the world, are still more appreciated than instructors who do not try humor. The bottom line is that people like humor; it enhances the learning environment and should be a staple of teachers.

There are numerous companies that have integrated humor into the everyday culture of the organization. Southwest Airlines may be the best example. Southwest Airlines' jokes and stories can be found all over the Internet (Rose, n.d., gosw.about.com/od/ resortsandtours/a/swjokes. htm). The humor of the company's flight attendants is more practiced than spontaneous. For example, one flight attendant can be heard saying, "We'll be dimming the lights in the cabin. Pushing the light-bulb button will turn your reading light on. However, pushing the flight-attendant button will not turn your flight attendant on." And this from another Southwest Airlines employee:

> Welcome aboard Southwest Flight XXX to YYY. To operate your seat-belt, insert the metal tab into the buckle, and pull tight. It works just like every other seatbelt, and if you don't know how to operate one, you probably shouldn't be out in public unsupervised. In the event of a sudden loss of cabin pressure, margarine cups will descend from the ceiling. Stop screaming, grab the mask, and pull it over your face. If you have a small child traveling with you, secure your mask before assisting with theirs. If you are traveling with more than one small child . . . pick your favorite.

Even pilots get into the act; one was overheard saying, "Weather at our destination is 50 degrees with some broken clouds, but we'll try to have them fixed before we arrive. Thank you, and remember, nobody loves you, or your money, more than Southwest Airlines" (Rose, n.d.).

Humor is not only used at Southwest Airlines, but it is one of the primary aspects of the airline's culture, from its president, Gary Kelly, to its more than 33,000 employees. Education can learn from Southwest Airlines. Just look at the company's mission statement: Creativity and innovation are encouraged for improving the effectiveness of Southwest Airlines.

## RESEARCH: ACADEMIC ACHIEVEMENT

Having fun is one thing, but school is about learning. Can humor help students learn? Numerous qualitative and quantitative studies indicate that humor enhances academic achievement. However, there are other studies explaining that humor has many other well-defined assets. My argument for using humor is similar to Pascal's wager about the existence of God. In essence, Pascal attempted to demonstrate that the only prudent course of action is to live as if God exists. In education the only prudent course of action is to use humor in school.

## INAPPROPRIATE USES OF HUMOR

Humor has to be used appropriately; hence one of the reasons for this book. Using a qualitative research design, Wanzer et al. (2006) examined the appropriate and inappropriate uses of humor. Wanzer found that inappropriate humor fell into four main categories: offensive humor (sexual jokes/comments, vulgar verbal expressions, drinking, drugs, or morbidity); disparaging humor with students as target (based on intelligence, gender, appearance, etc.); disparaging humor with "other" as target (using stereotypes in general, targeting gender, race, religion, etc.); and humor that disparages others. However, appropriate humor fell into four main categories:

1. Related humor: jokes, stories, critical/cynical examples, college life stereotypes, teacher performance, role-playing activities, creative language
2. Humor unrelated to class material: with the same subcategories
3. Self-disparaging humor: make fun of self, embarrassing stories, make fun of mistakes made in class, make fun of abilities (we are all broke; it is just at different levels)
4. Unintentional or unplanned humor

Inappropriate use of humor is similar to the admini-sphere, which may be defined as the rarified organizational layers beginning just above the rank and file in a school. Decisions that fall from the admini-sphere are often profoundly inappropriate or irrelevant to the problems they were designed to solve.

## GENDER DIFFERENCES

There are, however, many subtleties when using humor that define inappropriate and appropriate uses, for example, gender differences. Dr. Allan Reiss of the Stanford University School of Medicine reported in the *Proceedings of the National Academy of Sciences* that male and female brains react differently to humor: "Women appeared to have less expectation of a reward, which in this case was the punch line," so they were more pleased with humor (Azim, Mobbs, Jo, Menon, and Reiss, 2005). Women subject humor to more analysis with the aim of determining if the punch line was truly funny. Men are less discriminating and like one-liners more than women do: "The funnier the cartoon the more the reward center in the women's brain responded, unlike men who seemed to expect the cartoons to be funny from the beginning." In essence, women are more analytical and, therefore, do not expect the cartoons to be as funny as men do.

In order to illustrate these differences more graphically, figures 1.1 and 1.2 show pictorial descriptions of the female brain and the male brain.

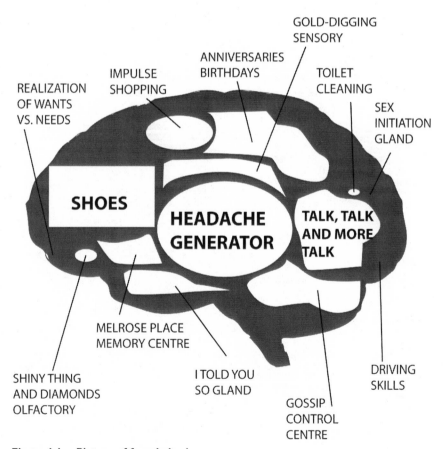

**Figure 1.1.   Picture of female brain**

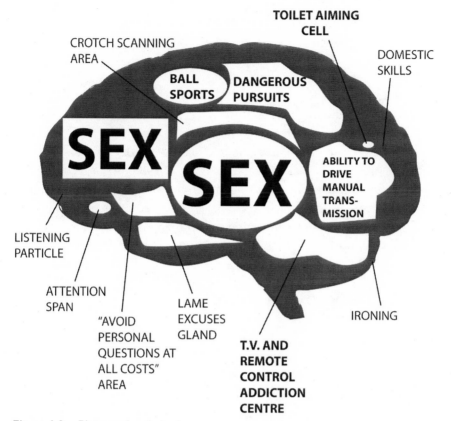

**Figure 1.2.    Picture of male brain**

## OUTLINE OF BOOK

Research students constantly ask me, "When do I know I am done researching?" The answer is always the same—"When I tell you." No, not really; the answer is that you are done when the same themes keep recurring in the analysis of the data, time and time again. Given this guideline, this book depicts a synthesis of the research on humor in the classroom, concluding that there are eight different categories where humor has a positive effect on the learning environment:

1. Culture and environment
2. Instruction

3. Relationships and teamwork
4. Communication
5. Stress
6. Creativity and divergent thinking
7. Student behavior
8. Teachers' interest at work

Consequently, each chapter in the book addresses one of the eight categories. Subsequently, each chapter has an introduction, a short section on research and theory supporting the strategy, action steps (including research results), and practical examples, that is, jokes, stories, puns, and humorous activities supporting the strategy. In the end, a summary pulls all the information together for review.

## RESEARCH: USED AND ABUSED

It is important to examine the research behind using humor in education. While this book emphasizes the practical components of using humor, these components are supported by research that has been conducted over the years. Because the conclusions in this book are based on research, it is only appropriate to define the term (a conclusion is the place where you got tired of thinking). It must be noted that there really is a plethora of quality (quantitative and qualitative) studies on the positive effects of using humor in teaching. So, the research had to be condensed. Listed below are the criteria used for selecting and using research studies in this book.

1. Both qualitative and quantitative studies were considered, but they had to be empirical in nature, for example, a solid research design followed by the collection of data. Literature reviews were used only if the essence of the article was to analyze and synthesize the material for solid data-based conclusions.
2. The study had to involve K–higher education, with the rare exception that a study focused on a business or health-care aspect directly related to the classroom, for example, improving the organization.

3. The study involved schools in the United States.
4. The study directly, or indirectly, examined the relationship of humor to the academic learning environment.
5. Humor was broadly defined, as was the academic learning environment.
6. Studies that contained effect sizes were emphasized, but they may be estimates in some cases. Not all researchers calculate effect size, and they certainly do not do so with a standard formula.
7. Of course, there exist many relevant studies that I did not include in this book because I found others that said the same thing but had a stronger research methodology, were written in a more concise manner, or simply were of a higher quality. For example, a dissertation with the same conclusions typically took precedence over an article in a periodical geared more toward the general public. Readers could probably argue about what studies should, or should not, have been included, but the conclusions should be similar.
8. Caveat to the above rules: if I thought it was funny, I included it; if I thought it made sense, I included it; and if it was just too good to leave out, I included it.

Much has been written about what is funny, how humor works, blah, blah, blah. Humor is different for different people. If it is funny, it is humor. Therefore, I have taken the shotgun approach in this study, to include more than less, in order to provide as many tools as possible for teachers and administrators.

# HUMOR BUILDS CULTURE IN SCHOOLS AND CLASSROOMS

Whether you think you can or think you can't, you're right.

—Henry Ford

Instructors who use humor, even if it is not the best humor in the world, are still more appreciated than instructors who do not try humor. The bottom line is that research tells us that people appreciate humor; it enhances the learning environment, students remember information more accurately, and there are many positive effects for the classroom.

Much has been written about improving the culture of an organization. There are how-to books and "field books" on how to create a learning organization, but one of the easiest aspects often overlooked is humor. (An invisible man marries an invisible woman. The kids were nothing to look at either.) For example, Bolinger (2001) studied 53 deans and 160 faculty in the American Assembly of Collegiate Schools of Business and found through statistical analysis a correlation between the attributes of humor and effectiveness in faculty members. Organizations are built on relationships and trust, so administrators should consciously encourage a climate of reciprocal humor as a means of reducing tensions. Humor should recognize the dignity of all individuals, demonstrating to employees that they can place confidence in the leader's objectivity and sense of justice, and thereby building trust. Humor is an aspect of attitudes and personality and should be used by leaders at all levels.

Think about it: after a great weekend, what is the first thing you do on Monday morning at school? Typically, individuals greet one another and then share experiences from the weekend. They tell each other jokes they heard on Saturday, talk about a movie they saw, or tell a funny story about their kids. You do not do this with strangers, but with your colleagues and friends as you build relationships with them. If everyone made of point of telling a humorous story to someone every Monday, or any other day, your group of friends would widen, relationships would build, and more trust would develop within the organization. You would be building a learning organization through humor.

Be sincere and knowledgeable with the content of your message and the associated humor. People are intelligent and can spot insincerity a mile away. In fact, meetings that are designed to improve the culture of an organization are like funerals: everyone gets all dressed up, no one wants to go but they have to, and when the meetings are done and the lights are turned off the attendees try to forget about them. Using humor to build culture is easy, fun, and supported by research.

## RESEARCH AND THEORY

You do not have to go far to find a book on how to improve the culture in an organization. However, a number of studies actually point to humor as a priority (e.g., Weise, 1996, and Kuiper, Grimshaw, Leite, and Kirsh, 2004). A comfortable learning environment is also a more effective learning environment. Bolinger (2001) completed survey research with a multiplicity of deans and faculty in the American Assembly of Collegiate Schools of Business and found a correlation between the attribute of humor and effectiveness in faculty members ($r = 0.538$) that equates to an effect size of 1.25, or close to a 40 percent gain in effectiveness. Torok, McMorris, and Wen-Chi (2004) found that students consider teachers using humor "entertaining" and "witty," which correlates with teachers' being competent.

Now, it must be noted that numbers are just numbers. ("I always find that statistics are hard to follow and impossible to digest. The only one

I can ever remember is that if all the people who go to sleep in church were laid end to end they would be a lot more comfortable." ~ Mrs. Robert A. Taft.) Nevertheless, the research does keep adding up.

It is not only that humor livens up the classroom, but it leads to more job satisfaction and a better learning environment, and students find the use of humor to be very important (Young, Whitley, and Helton, 1998). After all, the focus of any classroom should be the student. (On an interesting side note, Westcott [1983] found that while students enjoyed humor, there were statistically significant differences on humor scores between high-intelligence and low-intelligence students on standardized test scores. That is, high intelligence and high humor were correlated. If you are smart you have higher levels of humor.) However, humor always seems to be noted as providing a positive school environment.

## USE HUMOR TO IMPROVE LEADERSHIP

Warren Bennis is a noted author and researcher in the field of education (*On Becoming a Leader*, 1989). In 1996, Bennis wrote about Howard Gardner's research on the topic of leadership, noting that "the four factors Gardner lists as essential for effective leadership are a tie to a community or audience, a rhythm of life that includes isolation and immersion, a relationship between the stories leaders tell and the traits they embody, and arrival at power through the choice of the people rather than through brute force" (p. 3) and that "the right anecdote can be worth a thousand theories" (p. 3). For example, "If everything seems to be going well, you have obviously overlooked something."

It takes more than an anecdote to be a leader or teacher, but Ziegler, Boardman, and Thomas (1985) determined that cheerful, lighthearted humor was positively correlated with supportive leadership styles and a positive climate (as cited in Brooks, 1992, p. 15). (If you are motivated by a cute saying, you probably have a very easy job or you are ready to retire.) Dewey in 1910 understood that "to be playful and serious at the same time is possible, and it defines the ideal mental condition" (1997, p. 218). Mental keenness is a form of intellectual play that is needed. In fact, play may be a necessary piece of the whole child. The social brain finds another social brain in times of sorrow and joy (Dickmann and

Stanford-Blair, 2002). Schools are social places and while many schools are still working from the industrial model, Dewey (1916) argued that the school should be more like a family than a factory—providing a time for relating, learning, and laughing.

## Action Step I: Principals with a Sense of Humor Have a Positive Effect on Learning

Ziegler, Boardman, and Thomas (1985) concluded through empirical research that educational leaders can use humor to increase their effectiveness. The research demonstrates that there are significant relationships between certain humor factors and school climate. These same relationships exist between certain humor factors and leadership styles of principals perceived by teachers. The logical consequence of this research would seem to provide principals with an important reason for developing appropriate humor-related skills. This is especially important when coupled with the literature that concludes that leadership style is the salient factor that influences productivity and satisfaction of individuals in a school. Classes with teachers perceived as low in their overall use of humor were characterized as low in supportiveness, involvement, defensiveness, and innovation (Stuart and Rosenfeld, 1994).

## Practical Examples

If you are a sports fan, you can always depend on ESPN Classics to give you a great game. If you are a reader, the great classics in literature will never let you down, and if you are trying to use humor in the classroom, cartoons are the quintessential of "old reliable." Collect cartoons from the Internet, newspapers, and e-mails sent to you. Save them in a three-ring binder and use them, or scan them into your computer. I never view spam as a negative, but rather as an opportunity to find a joke to be used sometime in the future. For example, the two cartoons of the male and female brain in the introduction never fail to make a point and get a laugh. Here are some other general guidelines:

1. Humor increases interpersonal contact through eye-to-eye and face-to-face contact.

2. Humor creates a casual and safer atmosphere.
3. Adopt a laugh-ready attitude—it becomes contagious.
4. Provide humorous materials in any form to anyone.
5. Humor removes social inhibitions (Provine, 2000, pp. 210–14).

Remember to always abide by copyright laws—my lawyer friends tell me to include this line. For information, see www.lawyer-jokes.us/. Lawyers really are not so bad. Steven Wright suggests that only 99 percent of the lawyers give the rest a bad name.

Here is an example of a joke sent to me via the Internet years ago. I just keep this material and use it when trying to make a point to colleagues or friends.

A man piloting a hot-air balloon discovers he has wandered far off course and is hopelessly lost. He descends to a lower altitude and locates a man down on the ground. He lowers the balloon to within hearing distance and shouts, "Excuse me, can you tell me where I am?" The man below says: "Yes, you're in a hot-air balloon, about thirty feet above this field." "You must be a teacher," says the balloonist. "Yes, I am," replies the man. "And how did you know that?" "Well," says the balloonist, "what you told me is technically correct, but of no use to anyone." The man below says, "You must be a school principal." "I am," replies the balloonist. "How did you know?" "Well," says the man, "you don't know where you are, or where you're going, but you expect my immediate help. You're in the same position you were before we met, but now it's my fault!"

## Action Step 2: Promote Humor throughout the School to Build Culture and Leadership

Teachers and students laugh more in a group than by themselves. "Individuals laugh because of the social context or their relationship with other individuals. This is the base for social theorists who insist that laughter is primarily a method of dealing with the environment" (Hudson, 1979, p. 18). It only makes sense that the more you promote laughter in the class and in the school, the more connected teachers will be with teachers, students with students, and teachers with students. The use of humor actually symbolizes the culture of the organization and can be used to improve the overall school climate (Dandridge, Mitroff, and Joyce, 1980; Crawford, 1994b). Humor also has been linked directly with improving the effectiveness of leaders (Avolio, Howell, and Sosik, 1999; Crawford, 1994a).

## Practical Examples

If you take care of the little things, the larger problems disappear. Here are a few "little things" you can do to help change into a humor culture. (Change is inevitable, except from vending machines.)

1. Give small awards, or candy, at every meeting for the first to arrive, the best new idea, and so forth. We have a running joke in our department where if you present a creative new idea, "you are done for the month" and we say you no longer have to contribute. It is just a fun way to say thanks for the innovation.
2. Change the routine of your meetings by including amusing anecdotes and accounts of current happenings. Reverse the order of meetings from your typical sequence.
3. Add a timed "whine and cheese" item to the agenda. Use this time to celebrate accomplishments or discuss upcoming events.
4. Bring simple treats to meetings. People like to eat.
5. Use toys and props to loosen people up—the sillier the better. This sets the tone of the meeting or classroom.
6. Add a "rumor mill" to the end of each meeting to quash rumors and get issues and concerns on the table safely.
7. Instead of holding a meeting, watch an inspirational movie.
8. Try a stand-up meeting. Do not allow people to sit down; instead, they have to stand for the meeting. This will invoke conversation and you will be surprised how fast the meeting will end (Stephenson and Thibault, 2006, pp. 98–99).

## Action Step 3: Leaders Can Use Humor to Build Stronger Relationships and Be More Productive

Priest and Swain (2002) used two different studies to find that the "relation between leadership effectiveness and warm humorous style was a very strong one," while good leaders were rated higher in humor, even after controlling statistically for other attributes (p. 185). Specifically, school leaders benefit by using self-deprecating humor, thereby creating a more positive school climate. "If administrators and teachers can laugh at themselves, they'll be better able to get students to acknowledge their own shortcomings—and open the doors to more creative problem solving" (ASCD, 2001).

Using humor is not only fun for the students, but there is a direct correlation between using humor and being more productive. Philbrick (1989) found a statistically significant relationship between principals who appreciate humor and the ones who "get things done."

Ultimately, research suggests that humor helps to reveal, diagnose, and improve culture in an organization (Deal and Kennedy, 1999; Dwyer, 1991; Kahn, 1989). However, there has been some research that finds humor can serve as resistance and as a subversive tactic to the culture (Ackroyd and Thompson, 1999; Collinson, 1988, 2002; Linstead, 1985). The negative aspect of humor manifests mainly with put-down, aggressive, or insulting humor. Leaders must simply use common sense. Remember that when everything is coming your way, you are probably in the wrong lane.

## Practical Examples

As a teacher and/or leader, you can consciously misuse terms or clichés; this will instill a sense of superiority in students and staff, and maybe even a feeling of empathy for you.

1. Mispronounce a word on purpose, like saying "sandmich" instead of "sandwich" or "liberry" instead of "library."
2. Tape clever TV ads to be used as visual aids and inspiration.
3. Use cartoons in minutes of meetings, reports, and memos to support your ideas. Even Word art or clip art can be amusing in typical boring reports.
4. Develop patterns of humor at work, for example, running gags.
5. Find one person to be the good-humor man/woman—look for him or her to supply humor, but establish rapport so this person can be picked on.

6. Provide a positive reinforcement for using humor, for example, compliments, candy, and so on.

It is also important when you are hiring to look for individuals who have a sense of humor. This quality is often overlooked and certainly underrated. Humorous teachers and staff tend to be more creative and apt to accept change.

## Action Step 4: Effective Leaders Use Humor for Sustainability

Nadeau and Leighton (1996) analyzed data from the U.S. Department of Education on leadership in sustained school-improvement efforts and found that effective leaders cultivated a broad definition of community and gave voice to all stakeholders. Effective leaders were committed to the dream of continuous improvement and adopted key values; specifically, they used knowledge to minimize failure and they encouraged risk taking; demonstrated savvy and persistence; and put to use an array of personal characteristics (humor, passion, empathy, creativity, common sense, and patience). As Vince Lombardi never said, "Humor isn't everything, it is the only thing." Actually, humor isn't the only thing; it must be used in conjunction with many other disciplines and characteristics. More on this to come.

## Practical Examples

Do not reinvent the wheel. Save those "junk" e-mails with jokes, search the Internet, and use humorous websites. Two of the best sources are as follows: The Humor Project, www.humorproject.com, celebrated its thirtieth anniversary in 2007 and is filled with presentations, conferences, research, resources, and many other humorous references. The Association for Applied and Therapeutic Humor (AATH), www.aath.org, is an international community of professionals who incorporate humor into their lives. AATH is a leader in providing evidence-based information about current research and practical applications of humor.

## USE HUMOR TO IMPROVE ORGANIZATIONS

### Action Step 1: Allow Humor to Penetrate the Organization

Brooks (1992) summarizes the research of others by explaining that organizational humor, as a form of play, bonds people together, reduces conflict, creates new visions, and regenerates cultural values. Similarly, humor can assist organizational members in earning and maintaining a sense of social inclusion, especially by easing tension and boredom and by providing social rewards (Deal and Kennedy, 1982; Blau, 1963; Lundberg, 1969).

Humor needs to permeate your school. It needs to be allowed in the classroom, in the teachers' lounge, in the administrative offices, and even at school board meetings—however, school board members with a sense of humor just may be the ultimate oxymoron.

### Practical Examples

Not everyone is a comedian, and not everyone should try to be one— even some of the current comedians might want to find different jobs. The idea is not to be a stand-up comic/teacher, but rather to provide some humor in order to lighten the mood or just to set the tone of the day.

1. Try doing an impression of your favorite actor; it does not have to be perfect—just emphasize the mannerisms more than the voice.
2. Impersonations are the most sincere form of flattery. Let others try to impersonate you—it helps build camaraderie.
3. Funny noises or sounds are juvenile but funny. For example, use a duck call to get students' attention.
4. Slapstick humor is fun and easy. Pretend to trip, dropping your lesson plan or papers. Not everyone enjoys slapstick, but many do.
5. Smile more every day; it becomes contagious.
6. Have a dress-up day instead of casual Friday.
7. Make presentations, or run meetings, in costume.
8. Use humor in correspondence and even in announcements.
9. Tell stories about yourself. Sometimes the more humiliating, the funnier. They make you seem human.

10. Tell jokes, use mime, tell puns, riddles, satire, and parody. Look for humor in everything—reality is funnier than fiction. Listed below are examples of puns to use.

## Great, and Not-So-Great, Puns to Use

1. Déjà moo: the feeling that you've heard this bull before.
2. What do you call a fish with no eyes? A fsh.
3. Two fish swim into a concrete wall. The one turns to the other and says, "Dam!"
4. And finally, there was the person who sent twenty different puns to his friends, with the hope that at least ten of the puns would make them laugh. No pun in ten did.

## Action Step 2: Use Humor to Level the Playing Field at School

Gunning (2001) found that the use of humor in an organization was purposeful and served a number of psychological and social functions, including the following: reducing tension, entertaining, building rapport, sharing positive feelings, and controlling behavior. Antecedent conditions, such as physical appearance and personal regard, greatly impact humor. Moreover, the worker's rank in the hierarchy impacted how humor was created and experienced. Smith and White (1965) wrote in a literature review that humor appears to create within the corporate structure an amiable atmosphere that enhances employee performance. Humor can level the playing field by being an inclusive form of communication (e.g., Vinton, 1989). Ultimately, humor plays a role in socialization, communication and language, and organizational identity and commitment. Therefore, appropriate humor is seen as a principal characteristic in leadership.

### *Important Things Leaders Need to Know*

1. Age is a very high price to pay for maturity.
2. Going to church doesn't make you a Christian any more than standing in a garage makes you a car.
3. If you must choose between two evils, pick the one you've never tried before.

4. Not one shred of evidence supports the notion that life is serious.
5. It is easier to get forgiveness than permission.
6. Men are from Earth. Women are from Earth. Deal with it.
7. Opportunities always look bigger going than coming.
8. Experience is a wonderful thing. It enables you to recognize a mistake when you make it again.
9. By the time you can make ends meet, they move the ends.
10. Someone who thinks logically provides a nice contrast to the real world.

## Practical Examples

To change the culture of an organization, humor has to start at the top. The principal and/or superintendent needs to have a good sense of humor. At your weekly leadership team meeting, show a short, two- to three-minute video on the topic to be discussed. Go to YouTube.com to find something appropriate. It sets a new tone for the meeting.

## USE OF HUMOR IN THE CLASSROOM

### Action Step 1: Teachers Make the Difference in the Classroom

While there may be some contradictory evidence about the use of humor in the classroom, the use of appropriate humor is positively viewed by both teacher and student. Manning (2002) concluded that humor reduces stress, helps students master difficult information, develops higher-order thinking skills, and de-escalates tense situations. The more a teacher values humor, the more it is appreciated by the students. However, Manning found that students' value of classroom humor is significantly lower in urban than in suburban schools. And interestingly enough, he concluded that students value humor more with female teachers than male teachers. Female students value humor more than male students. Humor is like any new teaching strategy (differentiated instruction, new technology, direct instruction, and so forth): it does not make a bad teacher good, but it can make teachers more effective when used appropriately.

## Practical Examples

Allow humor to flow within the classroom and school. Promote the use of humor in the minutes of meetings and daily activities. Permit holidays to be celebrated with ornate costumes, plays, or activities brought forward by anyone within the organization. This helps make work more fun, but it is also the great equalizer. Principals at many schools have caught on to this fact when they have fun activities like pledging to milk a cow if 100 percent of the third graders reach a reading level or achieve a fund-raising goal. Put humorous signs on your door. Daily cartoons or acceptable drawings lighten up the atmosphere.

## Action Step 2: If Nothing Else, Students Like Teachers to Use Humor

OK, let's pretend for a minute that humor does not have any positive effect on academic achievement. Even if this were the case (and it is not), people simply like humor. Prosser (1997) used experimental research, with a sample of 210 adult students, to find the following:

1. More than 99 percent of the respondents reported humor as important in teaching adults.
2. Discussion and small groups are the most preferred methods for teaching with humor.
3. Attitude influences humor.
4. Instructors should be sensitive in using humor.
5. Age influences humor—younger faculty are more humorous.
6. Spontaneous humor is important—79 percent embrace this approach.
7. Approximately 80 percent said humor creates interest, 82 percent said humor helps with classroom participation, 80 percent said it keeps lectures from becoming boring, and 98.7 percent said humor increases rapport with students; while 24 percent use it to relax students, 67 percent said humor is motivating. Seventy-seven percent indicated that humor was a discussion starter. And finally, 64 percent prefer cartoons/comic strips, while 56.9 percent prefer jokes.

## Practical Examples

Friends tell one another stories and this builds a positive culture. So, you need to not only share a joke with friends but expand your realm of friends. As the principal, allow this type of activity to transpire. Begin conversations with a smile. Or you can take banana breaks—simply take a break in the middle of the day and everyone eats bananas that you bring in for the staff or class. For example, at a school meeting have individuals draw a picture of a vehicle that shows what the organization currently looks like and what it will look like in five years—the funnier and more unusual, the better. The pictures always prove to be conversation builders.

## Action Step 3: Humor Simply Is One Tool for Teachers

Wallinger (1997) found that humor is an excellent tool teachers can use to alleviate stress, improve communication, and defuse conflict. (Always keep your words soft and sweet, just in case you have to eat them.) On the other hand, Hurren (2001) indicated that when used wisely, humor in schools facilitates attention and motivation, improves teacher-student rapport, and makes all subjects more acceptable. Creating a humor-filled environment will engage students more in the subject matter and then make them more prone to higher achievement and fewer behavior problems. These are not contradictory results; instead, the data must be viewed as concluding that humor is simply one tool that teachers can use in a variety of ways, for a variety of effects. For example, there have been more than a few occasions when I have used a pair of pliers for home repair, knowing that it was the wrong tool, simply because I happened to have it in my hand at the time. Remember, everything looks like a nail when you have a hammer in your hand.

## Practical Examples

Have your staff read humorous books that have a message. Books like *Leadership by Attila the Hun, The Art of Being Lazy*, or any book by Scott Adams, the creator of *Dilbert*, can be both clever and informative.

You can always have individuals complete a fun questionnaire on their activities, favorite comedy shows, funniest story about themselves, funniest relative, and so forth. During meetings or a class allow individuals to read a funny, short story to lighten the mood. Funny questionnaires help you as a leader or teacher get to know your students and staff.

> A little girl was talking to her teacher about whales. The teacher said it was physically impossible for a whale to swallow a human because even though it was a very large mammal its throat was very small. The little girl stated that Jonah was swallowed by a whale. Irritated, the teacher reiterated that a whale could not swallow a human; it was physically impossible. The little girl said, "When I get to heaven I will ask Jonah." The teacher asked, "What if Jonah went to hell?" The little girl replied, "Then you ask him."

## Action Step 4: Using Humor on Tests Provides Positive Results

Ron Berk (2002) uses an interesting twist on his tests for college students. He includes humorous answers for many of the questions. For example, he may have a multiple-choice test with the typical possible answers of A, B, or C, but he will also include an option of D, Who cares? Using humor in testing and assessments gets the attention of students: they become more relaxed and actually learn the material in more detail (see also McMorris, Boothroyd, and Pietrangelo, 1997). Moreover, students strongly prefer the use of humor in tests (Berk, 2000; McMorris, Boothroyd, and Pietrangelo, 1997).

With any teaching technique, there are cautions. For example, Dickmeyer (1993) used a longitudinal content analysis from 1941 to 1991 to conclude that while there are benefits of humor, individuals need to be careful. Damaging humor can occur even after an open climate has been created. Guidelines for the use of humor in the classroom include:

1. Consider the teacher's presentational skills when planning the use of humor.
2. Consider the audience. Never insult an audience unless you know you have an excellent rapport with them.

3. Consider the course material when planning to use humor. Humor needs to connect to the material, and it cannot be sexually explicit, politically incorrect, or socially derogatory. Remember, your words must prove to be an improvement on the silence.
4. Practice the humor on colleagues or family members.

## Practical Examples

☺ Whenever I attend a meeting, class, or small gathering, I bring candy in a Harley-Davidson lunch box. The candy is awarded as prizes throughout the activity for good answers, for telling jokes, or just for interesting behavior. The lunch box is a great conversation piece.

☺ Begin each class with a humorous story, quote, top ten list, joke, or pithy saying. Look online to get a quote of the day. "Do not walk behind me, for I may not lead. Do not walk ahead of me, for I may not follow. Do not walk beside me, either. Just leave me alone." "The journey of a thousand miles begins with a broken fan belt and a leaky tire."

☺ Hold meetings at fun, off-campus locations, like a pancake house.

☺ Give fun, inexpensive prizes to students and staff for good ideas, comments, or even questions (Stephenson and Thibault, 2006, p. 98).

List of Several Pithy Sayings

1. They come for the chance to take chances, to make some unknowns known, to win without having to finish first.
2. How far can you go into the woods? Only half way because then you are going out.
3. If the horse is dead, dismount.
4. We all have the same twenty-four hours as Albert Einstein.

# ❸

# HUMOR IMPROVES
# CLASSROOM INSTRUCTION

In teaching, the greatest sin is to be boring.

—J. F. Herbart

**U**sing humor to improve classroom instruction is not only supported by research, but it has proven to be successful. It is also as simple as reading your e-mail. For example, you may have seen the following spam about a "real" answering machine message for a school.

> Hello! You have reached the automated answering service of your school. In order to assist you in connecting to the right staff member, please listen to all your options before making a selection: To lie about why your child is absent, press 1. To make excuses for why your child did not do his work, press 2. To complain about what we do, press 3. To swear at staff members, press 4. To ask why you didn't get information that was already enclosed in your newsletter and several flyers mailed to you, press 5. If you want us to raise your child, press 6. If you want to reach out and touch, slap, or hit someone, press 7. To request another teacher for the third time this year, press 8. To complain about bus transportation, press 9. To complain about school lunches, press 0. If you realize this is the real world and your child must be accountable and responsible for his or her own behavior, class work, and homework, and your child's lack of effort is not the teachers' fault . . . hang up and have a nice day!

Students appreciate humor, teachers like using it, and there are a myriad of studies showing the positive effects. For example, Thompson (2000) notes that people remember information associated with jokes because they have to pay more attention to humorous items in order to "get the joke."

It is actually easy to be funny, but the real question is, can students take notes from the information? After all, the point of using humor is to be a more effective teacher. This chapter explores why humor works in the classroom and how teachers can use it to improve academic achievement.

Before proceeding, we must note that there are three main guidelines to follow: practice, practice, practice (I know this is an old joke, but it fits here). Do not expect to be excellent the first time you try to be funny, but your comfort level will rise. Integrating humor is like driving a car: you certainly were not great the first time you sat behind the wheel, but after some practice in real situations you learned to drive—except if you are my neighbor's daughter, who drove into our tree the other day. I guess she thought the tree cut her off.

1. Humor should never be used to embarrass, ridicule, or otherwise harm a student.
2. Humor needs to be kept appropriate to the ability level of the students.
3. Humor should be intellectually challenging.

## LEARNING CURVE

As with anything, there is a learning curve in using humor. To start, read books (this book is, of course, the best possible source), and always have a thesaurus, rhyming dictionary, book of quotes, and clichés on hand. There are even good books (but not as good as this one) on funny hand-outs, how to be funny at the podium, and so forth.

## RESEARCH AND THEORY

Ron Berk is one of the leading researchers on using humor to improve academic achievement. He has conducted numerous experiments on the topic, including the use of humor on tests. For example, Berk computed ANCOVAs (analyses of covariance) to isolate the effects of humorous directions, humorous items, and the combination of both on emotional/physiological and worry/cognitive anxiety symptoms and biostatistics achievement (huh?). Basically, the use of humor on tests has the potential to lower anxiety and raise test scores by as much as 17 percent. ("Remember, there are two kinds of statistics, the kind you look up and the kind you make up." ~ Rex Stout.)

Mitchell (2005) supports Berk's conclusions. She used a mixed methodology to discover that humor works best on the younger employees, the under-twenty-five age group, but there are no differences based on race or location. In addition, she found that humor helps in getting the point across, keeping people's interest, and in remembering the content. On a different note, Thompson (2000) was able to use four different experiments to take humor to a more concrete level. She found that humor enhanced recall of information, regardless of whether the memory test occurred immediately or was delayed, concluding that students remember things longer when humor was used. Garner (2006) found similar conclusions. Students receiving humor in a lesson recalled, and retained, more information regarding the topic than did a group not receiving humor. However, you must remember that researching and doing are two different things. If we were taught how to fly the way we learn how to teach, we would have classes in the history of flying and statistics of flying but would probably never get off the ground. As with any research, this information does not provide teachers with a blank check. Humor does not work in every situation.

## USING HUMOR TO ENHANCE TEACHING AND LEARNING

Would you like your students more engaged in class, so they have increased retention of material? Humor can help. The right timing of humor, and the right amount of humorous events, establishes a balance of "fun" and "seriousness" in the classroom (Gurtler, 2002, p. 6). When a teacher connects humor to course material there is a building up of neural networks that have the potential to explode in a frenzy of learning for students (p. 6).

## Action Step 1: Humor Enhances both Teaching and Learning

First, let's get an overview of humor, teaching, and learning. Willard (2006) used a case study methodology to conclude that teachers using humor in their classes aid the learning process by

1. improving attitudes toward the subject, as well as decreasing anxiety, tension, stress, and boredom;
2. increasing comprehension, cognitive retention, interest, and task performance;
3. increasing motivation to learn and satisfaction with learning;
4. promoting creativity and divergent thinking. However, typically we do not "think out of the box"—we simply make the box bigger.

## Practical Examples

Try not to waste valuable class time on humor that is without a specific purpose. Connect humor to the material. Consider asking students to use humor in answering test questions. Students still need to answer the question, but they can be creative in the process. Another example of connecting humor to content is when I discuss using the Internet in research, I quote Dr. Seuss's *The Cat in the Hat* to explain how complex the process may be. (Dr. Seuss has numerous excellent lines that fit in the classroom.)

> So, as fast as I could,
> I went after my net, [for example, Internet]
> And I said, "With my net,"
> I can get them I bet,
> I can get those Things yet.

## Action Step 2: Humor Enhances both Teaching and Learning by Improving Attention, Motivation, and Rapport with Students

Don't be afraid to joke around with students. Hurren (2001) found that when used wisely, humor facilitates attention and motivation, improves teacher-student rapport, and makes all subjects more acceptable.

Creating a humor-filled environment will help students be more interested in the subject matter and in turn raise achievement and decrease behavior problems.

Specifically, using humor three to four times per class for high school students is appropriate. There are negative effects of using too much humor. Teachers lose competence and respect of the perceptive students and may even become class clowns if they overdo it (Ziv, 1988).

## Practical Examples

As noted previously, Berk has been studying humor for some time, but more importantly, he blends research with practice. His website, www.ronberk.com/html/articles.html, is filled with practical ideas and supporting research. Listed below are key points about using humor.

1. Students view humor as an effective teaching tool to facilitate learning.
2. Strategies for using humor must be well planned and executed systematically to achieve specific outcomes.
3. Both content-specific and generic humorous material tailored to the characteristics of each class can be effective in appropriate applications. Get to know your class; give them a humor quiz to find out their likes and dislikes and what they find funny. Personalize the humor, that is, use differentiated humor.
4. Humor tends to be more effective when two or more of the senses, especially visual and aural (written and oral), are involved.
5. Offensive humor should never be used in the classroom.
6. The strategies for using humor are adaptable and can be generalized to any discipline and course content.

## Action Step 3: Use Humorous Readings to Increase Retention of Material

Many teachers have found the comic appeal of literature. Students enjoy being part of an audience when humorous literature is shared. Moreover, jokes and funny literature that challenge the individual's intellectual capabilities will allow for growth and are appreciated most by students (Klesius, Laframboise, and Gaier, 1998). In addition to being linked to intellectual stimulation, humorous literature has been associated with increased enjoyment, increased situational interest, and improved attention or learning (Sheppard, 2002).

Remember being a sixth grader and having to take a human sexuality class? You used to talk big, but in reality knew very little—some of us still know very little on the topic. Reading and learning about sexuality, especially at that age, creates discomfort and embarrassment for many. Vogel (1995) found that the use of humor relieves tension, enhances memory, increases class interest, masks embarrassment, heightens self-efficacy, and fosters group cohesion in a human sexuality class. Now we have a real practical application for humor. Every school or program has at least one course that students dread taking, for whatever reason. Many times in college, this course is statistics. Most of our students call it Sadistics. Of course, students think statistics have all the virtues they dislike and none of the vices they admire. Berk (1996) found that the benefits of humor in teaching college statistics include: reducing tension, boredom, stress, and anxiety while improving attitude toward the subject; as well as increasing comprehension, interest, and task performance. I use a YouTube video with high school students rapping about how to use statistics in life, and it is only three minutes long. In addition, humorous textbooks are helpful.

## Practical Examples

Books are obviously one of the most important aspects of education, possibly second only to the teachers themselves. Why not find books that are both informative and entertaining?

- ☺ Include examples of regional literature in thematic units.
- ☺ Use funny textbooks, like *Statistics with a Sense of Humor*, by Fred Pyrczak, or *Statistics for People Who (Think They) Hate Statistics*, by Neil Salkind. In fact, Pyrczak Publishing has numerous quality textbooks with added humor.
- ☺ Keep a book of jokes or cartoons handy and read something funny ten minutes before teaching a class or attending a meeting. It puts you in the right mood for class. If you start "losing" the class, just have a joke break and read from the book.

## USING HUMOR TO ENHANCE TEACHING

### Action Step 1: Humor Adds to the Appeal of Teachers

Let's face it, teachers typically like being the center of attention by being in front of class. So, it only makes sense that they like being funny because the frequency and use of humor correlates positively to perceived appeal, effectiveness, and delivery of information. The bottom line is that humor in teaching has tangible benefits. Interestingly enough, years ago, researchers would say that male teachers who used humor received higher evaluations than female teachers (Bryant, Comisky, Crane, and Zillmann, 1980, p. 515). However, most authors today indicate that there is essentially no difference between male and female teachers using humor (Manning, 2002; Ramirez, 2002).

### Practical Examples

Ten items for using humorous material for class.

1. Use humorous material on syllabi, for example, cartoons, clip art, funny sayings—"Indecision is the mother of flexibility."
2. Use pretend descriptors, cautions, and warnings on the covers of handouts, such as *"Do not* fold, mutilate, or spindle," or "Close cover before striking."
3. Use an opening joke to motivate students, to serve as a release valve for stress, and to trigger a fun attitude toward learning.
4. Use skits and dramatizations. Find a character with whom the students can relate and develop a short skit based on the character that can lead into the presentation. The funny part is the parody.
5. Spontaneous humor has three subcategories: (a) response to students' questions (ad-libs), (b) response to the professor's mistake, and (c) response to interruption. Memorize a few ad-libs, like saying, "Thanks for the input, but you have to remember *I* give out the grades in this class." Say it with a smile.
6. Use humorous questions. Present the material and ask how many of the students don't care.
7. Use humorous examples. This may be hypothetical or an ironic twist to a serious example; for instance, use local sports teams,

plays, activities of students, and silly homecoming floats in your examples.

8. Use humorous problem sets. These are similar to humorous examples and can supplement typical textbook problems.
9. Use games in class, for example, do *Jeopardy*-type review for exams.
10. Use humorous material on exams. Maybe use funny titles, directions, test items, or possible extra credit (Berk, 1996).

## Action Step 2: Humor Is Not the Simple Answer

Several authors have theorized that humor can reduce anxiety and make learning easier, but the connection can be complex. The use of humorous examples in class can reduce anxiety and produce better test results, but the effect depends on the students' levels of intelligence and/or anxiety. The higher the level of intelligence, the higher the effect of humor, but higher levels of anxiety lead to lower effects of humor. For example, if the student is intelligent and does not experience test anxiety, humor should aid more in the learning process (Edwards and Gibboney, 1992, pp. 17–18).

This situation can get even more complex because some researchers conclude that students find humorous presentations less believable than nonhumorous presentations, but indicate they learn more from the humorous lessons. Nevertheless, students indicate higher levels of interest and a more positive attitude toward the content of humorous presentations (Tribble, 2001); that is, students pay attention.

## Practical Examples

☺ People love trivia, and it is quite easy to find and use. For example, the websites www.funtrivia.com and www.trivia.com provide many great examples. (The king of hearts is the only king in a deck of cards without a mustache. Venus is the only planet that rotates clockwise—since Venus is normally associated with women, what does this tell us?)

☺ Use interesting oxymorons, for example, State worker, legally drunk, exact estimate, funny professor.

☺ The same jokes or humorous activities that work for elementary students do not work for adults. You need to have an "arsenal" of jokes, puns, overheads, activities, and so on.

☺ Carry around a supply of lists to be used at the right time.

☺ Use historical and clever sayings to make a point. For example, here are a few that almost everyone should be able to relate to. Use them in an unusual manner or to start a story.

1. Fourscore and seven years ago . . .
2. I'll be back [in the voice of Arnold Schwarzenegger].
3. I shall return. . . .
4. Here's looking at you, kid.

Interchange words to help sell your point: "Ask not what you can do for humor, ask what humor can do for you." Of course, the phrases you use should depend on the average age of the audience.

### More Pithy Sayings to Memorize and Use "Spontaneously"

1. Always remember you're unique, just like everyone else.
2. Never test the depth of the water with both feet.
3. It may be that your sole purpose in life is simply to serve as a warning to others.
4. It is far more impressive when others discover your good qualities without your help.
5. If you tell the truth you don't have to remember anything.
6. If you haven't much education you must use your brain.
7. Never mess up an apology with an excuse.
8. Never underestimate the power of stupid people in large groups.
9. Good judgment comes from bad experience and a lot of that comes from bad judgment.
10. Timing has an awful lot to do with the outcome of a rain dance.
11. Telling a man to go to hell and making him do it are two entirely different propositions.
12. Never miss a good chance to shut up.
13. Generally speaking, you aren't learning much when your mouth is moving.

14. Anything worth taking seriously is worth making fun of.
15. Experience is something you don't get until just after you need it.

## Action Step 3: Interesting Research Findings Concerning Humor

There is a link between humor and use of metaphors in learning. The use of metaphors can increase retention by 40 percent (Glenn, 2002). For the best results with learning, use humor that is intellectually challenging, rather than a base level of humor that all students will readily understand (Rareshide, 1993, p. 20). Moreover, "teachers recommend that humor should be spontaneous and that it should only be used when it comes naturally and fits the teacher's personality" (Rareshide, 1993, p. 20). Cartoons always seem to work. The use of cartoons does two things: (1) it shows students in a comfortable, familiar way that background knowledge is necessary if you are going to get the most enjoyment out of life, and (2) you have to read to get the knowledge, that is, cartoons provide graphic clues along with the printed material and they unlock the unknown meaning of words (Guthrie, 1999, p. 2).

## Practical Examples

☺ Constantly search for amusing anecdotes that can be used to illustrate difficult concepts. Keep a journal with you at all times to write down ideas as you see or hear them. Of course, you can also use technology to take notes with a PDA or cell phone for recordings and pictures.

☺ Utilize analogies that transform abstract ideas into more familiar examples. To teach regression in statistics, I use the example of how students make decisions in presidential elections.

☺ Use homemade "props" to communicate important ideas. Props can be used over and over again. For example, full-size head shots of historical figures on a sign with a stick may seem corny, but they get students' attention.

## Action Step 4: Humor Increases the Interest of the Teacher/Speaker

It has been said that a well-developed sense of humor is a priceless asset (Nadeau and Leighton, 1996, p. v). This priceless asset produces more positive reactions from the audience (students) toward the speaker. It also enhances interest in the speech, or lesson plan, and effectiveness of persuasive speeches (Gruner, 1985; Crawford, 1994b). Course materials are more attention getting, original, and likable when mixed with humor (Michaels, 1998).

### Practical Examples

Identifying similarities and differences is a proven method of successful teaching. Integrating humor makes the technique even more important. For example, the hammer Michelangelo used to create *Pietà* was similar to the one used to destroy it. By the same token, there is more information in one edition of the *New York Times* today than any one person would have received in an entire lifetime in seventeenth-century England.

## USING HUMOR AS A TEACHING TOOL TO ENHANCE LEARNING

### Action Step 1: Why to Use Humor as a Teaching Tool

Humor can be used as a rhetorical strategy for teachers or it can be used simply to get the students' attention (Boland and Hoffman, 1982; Bricker 1980; Brooks, 1992). Humor can also enhance the classroom environment and it has been shown to increase attendance (Devadoss and Foltz, 1996; Romer, 1993; White, 1992). Interestingly, humor "helps to draw and hold the child's attention." "The effectiveness of nonrelevant humor diminishes with a person's age so that by adulthood, nonrelevant humor is not only not acceptable, but can even hinder the acquisition of information" (Coleman, 1992, p. 272).

## Action Step 2: Humor Appears to Increase Your Memory and Judgment of Learning

Researchers have found that the use of humorous cartoons appears to support good memory performance (Schmidt and Williams, 2001; Wierzbicki and Young, 1978). Jennifer Thompson (2000) explored the effects of humor and delayed testing on memory and metamemory performance. She used experimental research to conclude that over time, humor increased how much people thought they remembered (see also Ziv, 1988; Townsend et al., 1983).

We are all born with a sense of humor; it just develops differently in each of us. People appreciate funny things and want to be in a humorous environment, but it is up to the teacher to use humor so it works in the class. The psychological mechanisms that comprise a sense of humor are different in each one of us, as different personalities play a role in the appreciation of humor. People have different personalities, they have different senses of humor, and the effect of humor in the classroom varies. Do not be discouraged. Try different types of humor in different

Figure 3.1.   Always give 100 percent at work

situations to see which one works. And above all else, get to know your students.

## PRINCIPLES FOR USING HUMOR IN THE CLASSROOM

Teachers can encourage laughing at humorous circumstances to build a feeling of unity. They can also use humorous examples and present concepts to help students comprehend and retain material. For example, when I teach research, I use data from the Green Bay Packers for students to analyze. Knowing your students and playing to their beliefs and likes is important. Every group has its special traditions. Use this information to build bonds. In Wisconsin, the Green Bay Packers are second only to—nothing.

> John Elway, after living a full life, died. When he got to heaven, God was showing him around. They came to a modest little house with a faded Broncos flag in the window. "This house is yours for eternity, John," said God. "This is very special; not everyone gets a house up here." John felt special, indeed. On his way up the porch, he noticed another house just around the corner. It was a three-story mansion with a Green and Gold sidewalk, fifty-foot-tall flagpole with an enormous Packers logo flag. John looked dismayed and said, "God, I'm not trying to be ungrateful, but I have a question. I was an all-pro QB, I won two Super Bowls, and I even went to the Hall of Fame. So, why does Bart Starr get a better house than me?" God chuckled, and said "John, that's not Bart Starr's house, it's mine."

Staying on the sports theme, the rivals of Wisconsin Cheeseheads are the Minnesota Vikings and Chicago Bears.

> Three guys, a Vikings fan, a Packers fan, and a Chicago Bears fan are out walking together one day. They come across a lantern and a genie pops out. "I will give you each one wish; that's three wishes total," says the genie.
> The Vikings fan says, "I am a farmer, my dad was a farmer, and my son will also farm. I want the land to be forever fertile in Minnesota." With a blink of the genie's eye, POOF—the land in Minnesota was forever made fertile for farming. The Bears fan was amazed, so he said, "I want a wall

around Illinois, so that no infidels, or Packers fans, can come into our precious state." Again, with a blink of the genie's eye, POOF—there was a huge wall around Illinois. Izzy, the Wisconsinite, asked, "I'm very curious. Please tell me more about this wall." The genie explained, "Well, it's about 150 feet high, 50 feet thick, and 1,200 miles long, and it completely surrounds the state; nothing can get in or out." Izzy said, "Fill it up with water."

I use this joke when discussing simple descriptive statistics to calculate the size and strength of the wall.
Words of advice:

1. Humor should be appropriate to the situation and contain the personality of the instructor or students. You must be yourself. Students and peers will see through fake enthusiasm.
2. Teachers may not want to use humor in high-anxiety-producing situations.
3. The target of humor should be something, or someone, other than students.
4. If you are a competent instructor or leader, and gain the respect of students, self-disparaging humor can work very well. It makes the instructor more personable.
5. Even though humor that has female targets may be perceived as funnier than humor that has male targets, caution should be used not to perpetuate sexist notions. (This is actually true of any subject. In today's politically correct mania, every topic must be considered carefully before being part of humor.) For example, on YouTube there is a video of Hillary Clinton at a town-hall meeting with a young man interrupting her speech by yelling, "Iron my shirts, Iron my shirts." Some may find this video insulting, even if others find it humorous.
6. Teachers who establish high immediacy through behaviors other than humor may not want to use a high degree of storytelling because it may be seen as a digression.
7. Teachers can use funny stories related to the topic to improve the overall attitudes of students.
8. To be perceived as effective by students, instructors should use humor that adds to the content of education and contributes to the point (Edwards and Gibboney, 1992, pp. 22–23).

Therefore, research has shown that using humor in the classroom improves classroom instruction. However, you need to keep it simple, make your point, get in and get out, and always keep it connected to the content.

1. How do you put a giraffe into a refrigerator?

   Answer:

   Open the refrigerator and put in the giraffe, and close the door.

   This question tests whether you tend to do simple things in an unduly complicated way. When dealing with humor in the classroom, keep it simple—do not overthink the concept.

2. How do you put an elephant into a refrigerator?

   Did you say, "Open the refrigerator, put in the elephant, and close the refrigerator?" This is incorrect.

   Correct answer:

   Open the refrigerator, take out the giraffe, put in the elephant, and close the door.

   This tests your ability to think through the repercussions of your previous actions. When using humor, take a minute or two to think about the joke. Can it offend someone? Does it fit the material?

3. The Lion King is hosting an animal conference. All the animals attend except one. Which animal does not attend?

   Answer: The elephant does not attend because he is in the refrigerator—remember, you just put him there.

   This question tests your memory. In using humor in the classroom, you need to remember which jokes you told, which ones worked, and which ones did not. Using the same stale jokes, class after class, will produce more negative effects than positive.

4. There is a river you must cross but it is inhabited by crocodiles. How do you manage to cross?

   Answer:

   You swim across, because all the crocodiles are attending the animal conference.

   This tests whether you learn quickly from your mistakes. Integrating humor into the classroom will produce mistakes (just like trying a new lesson plan or any other teaching technique). Don't worry, just learn from your mistakes and move on.

**4**

# HUMOR BUILDS
# RELATIONSHIPS AND TEAMWORK

The main thing about the main thing is that it is to be kept as the main thing.

**W**hen relationships improve, teaching improves (Fullen, 2001). Humor increases relationships, so therefore, it should logically mean that humor improves teaching and learning. As noted previously, "Laughter is only rarely a response to jokes. It is, instead, the quintessential human social signal. It solidifies relationships and pulls people into the fold" (Provine, 2000, as cited in Begley, 2000, p. 76). "Laughter seems intimately en-twined with our physiology. It blocks a neural reflex that regulates muscle tone, proving the 'going weak with laughter' is more than a metaphor" (Begley, 2000, p. 76). Humor helps teachers gain approval from students, it reinforces group relationships, and it builds trust within schools. By the way, I do not subscribe to the philosophy that "teamwork is a lot of people doing what I say."

## RESEARCH AND THEORY

Bryant, Comisky, Crane, and Zillmann (1980) studied behaviors exhib-ited by teachers in presenting their lesson plans. A sample of sessions of undergraduate courses was tape-recorded by enrolled students. The researchers also utilized field observations and student questionnaires in order to evaluate the relationship between humor use and perceived effectiveness of teachers. They concluded that students find teachers using humor to be more appealing, competent, and effective in their delivery. They also gave higher evaluations to teachers who used humor, with effective sizes ranging from 0.10 (small) to 0.19 (medium).

## Action Step 1: Get to Know Your Students

Many experts contend that the connection between the instructor and the student is the key to learning. Effective teachers are enthusiastic and have a strong sense of humor, which develops a positive learning environment (Pollio and Humphreys, 1996; Lowman, 1994). In addition, teaching effectiveness is enhanced by the use of appropriate humor, which develops mutual respect, reduces anxiety, and has a positive effect on test performance (Kher, Molstad, and Donahue, 1999; Bryant, Comisky, Crane, and Zillmann, 1980).

In order to use humor appropriately, you must first do your homework. Get to know your students. Listen to what they are saying and talking about. Remember, from listening comes wisdom and from speaking comes repentance. You can give students a little quiz to find out their likes, dislikes, what they do during their spare time, and so on. Make notes on what they find funny and what they do not. Do not be afraid to even ask people if something is funny. I realize that I may be a techno geek (*not* a nerd), but I keep a database of jokes and record reactions of my audiences.

## Practical Examples

- ☺ Do not be afraid to laugh at yourself. In fact, laugh with your students. Such laughter helps to promote a bond between a teacher and students. Laughter is contagious.
- ☺ Cooperative learning is not only a great teaching technique but also a wonderful opportunity to integrate humor. Allow students to deliver funny PowerPoint presentations, skits, or comedy parodies of famous shows, for example, *Saturday Night Live*. As teams work together, allow the students to freely use humor. Remem-

ber that bearing a child takes nine months, no matter how many people you assign to the task.

☺ What is greater than God, the poor have it, the rich need it, and if you eat it you will die? [Nothing.]

## Action Step 2: Field-Test Your Material—Look Spontaneous and Be Prepared

While successful classroom instruction involves good teaching, there are other factors that engage students. Field-test the material before using it. You may want to find a colleague or friend to try your jokes out on. Go around testing out stories, jokes, and activities on your family. If it is funny to a select few, it should work with your class or colleagues. (If they find the joke funny, use it. If they do not find the joke funny, find new friends.)

### Practical Examples

☺ Leaders who use humor seem more part of the group, more accessible, and more approachable. Learning to integrate humor is like riding a bike: you may fall down a few times at first, but once you figure it out, it comes easily. Nevertheless, there are lots of "training wheels" to help with the process. For example, the four-CD set entitled *Learn How the Pros Make 'em Laugh*, hosted by Darren LaCroix, is a great learning tool.

☺ Try using cartoons on bathroom or office passes.

☺ There are a host of good movies to use in class: *School of Rock, Napoleon Dynamite, Tommy Boy, Ferris Bueller's Day Off, Shrek*. You do not have to show the entire movie; small clips from each one will make the point. For example, use the scene in *Ferris Bueller* where Ben Stein, as an economics teacher, lectures to a class in a monotone: "Anyone? Anyone?" This is a great teaching tool on how not to teach.

☺ Watch funny television comedies—in class and outside of class, this can build relationships. "Relationships are hard. It's like a full-time job, and we should treat it like one. If your boyfriend or girlfriend wants to leave you, they should give you two weeks' notice. There should be severance pay, and the day before they leave you, they should have to find you a temp." ~ Bob Ettinger.

## Action Step 3: Use Humor That Is Practical

To be most effective, humor needs to be real, simple, and practical. The four-part quiz on page 41 can help with these concepts. (You have all seen this floating around the Internet. It is a good example of saving those dumb jokes sent out constantly on the Internet because they may come in handy someday.) Moreover, you can use this quiz with many different topics—just make a few adjustments in the analysis.

One easy way to incorporate practicality into humor is to focus on common experiences or things that your students or colleagues consider an annoyance. Everybody loves to know they are not alone in their complaints—this is why we have the U.S. government. It is not so much the joke but more that teachers show a sense of humor and are prepared (Wilkins, 2006).

## Action Step 4: Always Relate the Humor to the Material

According to Brooks (1992), Pollio and Bainum (1983) note that:

joking and laughing can be seen as attempts to reaffirm common bonds of a group or relieve tensions and thereby allow the group to work more effectively. Second, humor can distract a group from its task by calling attention to some specific tension in the group or to the person making the remark. However, they found that humorous behaviors do not necessarily interfere with a group's task effectiveness. Pollio and Bainum determined that if a humorous remark was related to the problem, it served to facilitate task completion; irrelevant witty remarks distracted the group, however, and decreased efficiency. (Brooks, 1992, p. 16)

Always relate humor to the audience. This means that you need to do some homework. What age are your students or staff? What are they talking about or complaining about? Talk with students ahead of time to find out what is on their minds. Be sure to read the room. If people are not paying attention, notice this fact and move on to something else. This means that you really need to plan several jokes ahead of time.

Write jokes, stories, or activities into the lesson plans so you do not forget where to use them. Doing this helps you keep track of which ones you use so you do not repeat the same jokes.

## Practical Examples

☺ Laughing at yourself will help build relationships with students by reinforcing their effort and providing recognition. It also is a form of cooperative learning and even providing feedback.

☺ As a leader, try to joke equally with everyone. If you have a favorite person to joke around with, it will be viewed as favoritism. By including everyone, a broader and deeper culture will be developed within the organization. I actually keep my class list next to me and check off the names of students as I joke with them.

☺ Laugh at yourself when you make mistakes. This will not only open the culture but help empower learners.

☺ Have students bring in jokes to start the class. Before you start class, have one person read a joke. It really assists the learning if you can have a discussion on how the joke relates to the course content. Humor can break cultural and gender barriers. It tends to make the world smaller and more intimate. Here is an example: A kindergarten teacher was observing her classroom of children while they drew. She would occasionally walk around to see each child's work. As she got to one little girl named Ceci who was working diligently, she asked what the drawing was. Ceci replied, "I'm drawing God." The teacher paused and said, "But no one knows what God looks like." Without missing a beat or looking up from her drawing, the girl replied, "They will in a minute."

## Action Step 5: Include Students in the Joking Process

Be sure to include students in the joking process. Humor has been found to be beneficial to establishing caring relationships between teachers and students, but just like any relationship, using humor cannot be one-sided. Pedde (1996) found such relationships to be critical to the engagement of students in the classroom. However, this means that students need to be engaged. You can engage students by conversing with them. Make them part of the teaching activities. Joke about the things you know and things that the students know so they can take ownership of the material. For example, you can have a "joke board" where students can post funny cartoons or jokes related to the course material.

## Practical Examples

☺ Have two or three group exercises memorized or written on a 3 × 5 card so you can refer to them at any time, or store the exercises in a PDA. This book provides just a few examples; there are countless resource books with entertaining activities such as *Playing Along* by Izzy Gesell or *A Handbook of Interactive Exercises for Groups* by Barlow, Blythe, and Edmonds.

☺ Tape a piece of paper on everyone's back with a joke written on it. Put the punch line on someone else's back. Have the group members walk around reading one another's backs to see where the joke fits the punch line.

☺ Humor can unite members of a group and help them persevere in even mundane tasks (Wallinger, 1997). Have a humor board at work or in the classroom. Allow individuals to bring in funny stories from the newspapers. You would be surprised to see the number of unusual or humorous situations people get into.

☺ Be sure to openly share your sense of humor.

## Action Step 6: Build a Culture of Humor in Your Classroom

Humor sets a positive social context for teachers and students to build relationships. Humor helps build trust and can invoke feelings of belonging and personal value to the group. These friendships and relationships are all key to better learning. This means that the more students get to know one another and the teacher, the more they will joke around and build stronger relationships (Brown, Dixon, and Hudson, 1982; Chapman, 1974; Malpass and Fitzpatrick, 1959; Neuendorf and Fennel, 1988).

Reynolds and Nunn (1997) conducted a study on two sites with more than eight hundred students and thirty-six instructors. The two researchers identified instructors as having strong teaching reputations. All groups of students identified instructor criticisms and put-downs as discouraging engagement. Female freshmen described the use of humor as significantly more likely to encourage participation than did freshman males. Upperclassmen and their instructors agreed in rating praise, use of humor, supportive atmosphere, use of student ideas, and use of student names as strong factors encouraging student participation. Undergraduates at all levels reported the use of humor as a stronger encourager of class participation.

As a teacher, you need to be able to speak the same language as students; however, be careful to "speak softly and carry a big joke."

1. Allow students to enjoy your presence and personality.
2. Revealing your humor will get students' attention.
3. Use self-deprecating humor—it levels the playing field.
4. Capitalize on unexpected funny moments.
5. Don't worry about looking silly—students like teachers who try humor and fail more than they like teachers who do not try humor (Stephenson and Thibault, 2006, p. 59). Think of it this way: Dave Barry wrote that "you can say any foolish thing to a dog, and the dog will give you a look that says, 'My God, you're right! I never would've thought of that!'"

### Action Step 7: Humor Can Be Used to Build Norms and Expectations in Class

"The expression of humor in groups reduces anxieties and hostilities and fosters rapport, personal attraction, and group solidarity. Joking is a powerful tactic to reinforce group norms, morality, values, power status, and existing ideology" (Wilson, 1999, p. 231). However, it must be noted that humor can be viewed as both a lubricant and as an abrasive in social interactions. It can be used to facilitate social interaction and to keep conversations moving freely, or it may cause interpersonal friction that can modify the nature of the interaction (Martineau, 1972; Malone, 1980). Remember, the sword that is used to point can also be used to cut.

While many researchers have written that humor can involve superiority over other individuals in a group (Hudson, 1979; Meyer, 1990), humor can also diminish hierarchy and status differentiation (Duncan, 1982). Managers also signal their availability and trust through joking (Vinton, 1989). So, in addition to improving the popularity and influence of the speaker (Gruner, 1965a, 1965b), humor can be used to improve the environment and cope with an ambiguous situation, and can play on the positively balanced relationship between person, group, and joke (Hudson, 1979; Goldstein, 1976).

## Practical Examples

☺ Teachers need to model humor for students and allow them to bring in their own jokes. You should even allow time in class for jokes. This will establish an environment that builds trust (Stephenson and Thibault, 2006, p. 65).

☺ Schedule regular school spirit days and allow the students to make the plans—with humor and within reason.

☺ Offer students cocurricular activities other than team sports. Have unusual activities, like Lego building.

☺ Start a comedy club for students.

☺ Arrange a few occasions each year for students and staff to mix socially (Stephenson and Thibault, 2006, p. 64).

☺ Hold a schoolwide contest to match staff members to their baby pictures.

☺ Create a secret buddy system to perform a random act of fun.

☺ Encourage staff members to think of small ways to make one another smile.

☺ Invite former and retired staff members and school board personnel to special occasions.

☺ Send a "bouquet-of-hour flowers" to a staff member with a note that says to enjoy the flowers for one hour and then send them on.

☺ Host a film festival of comedies at lunchtime.

☺ Make sure to express your appreciation to those very special staff members blessed with a sense of humor (Stephenson and Thibault, 2006, p. 94).

## USING HUMOR TO BUILD TEAMWORK

In addition to being able to build relations, humor can also improve teamwork. The reduction of social distance typically is expressed in terms of group cohesiveness. Numerous research studies have examined the role of humor in developing cohesion among group members (Brooks, 1992, p. 13).

Pogrebin and Poole (1988) presented three functions of humor that operate to build and maintain group cohesiveness. First, humor allows group members to share common experiences and to probe the attitudes, perceptions, and feelings of other group members in a nonthreatening manner. Humor helps to translate an individual's concern into a group issue, thus reinforcing group solidarity. Second, humor promotes social solidarity through the mutual teasing which allows group members to realize that they share a common perspective. This "laughter of inclusion," as well as humor aimed at people outside the group, helps to define social boundaries. Third, groups utilize humor as a coping strategy in managing a variety of forces beyond their direct control. (Brooks, 1992, p. 13)

### Practical Examples

☺ Allow students to hand in cartoons along with their homework or to replace one set of assignments per semester.

☺ Have a treat day or ask students if they want to bring in treats— the older the student, the better with this one—even in college. Food may not be funny, but it does lighten the atmosphere.

☺ Keep a communal photo album or scrapbook of students.

☺ Post a funny door sign to let students know how approachable you are. Allow students to post cartoons on their desks or name tags.

☺ Display humorous posters, pictures, or props in the classroom or in the hallways.

☺ Keep a supply of funny stickers to give out on assignments or tests, or just in class.

☺ Maintain a master calendar with birthdays and other events. Find ways to celebrate, especially with fellow teachers (Stephenson and Thibault, 2006, p. 97).

## Action Step 1: Allow Students Time to Joke with One Another in Small Groups

In today's classroom, much of the research points to the use of teams or small-group work to enhance the learning. This is fine, but we all know that assigning students (or even adults) to small groups causes disagreements to erupt. There are undoubtedly many conflict-resolution strategies to employ, but nondirected humorous remarks provide a group with a brief respite needed to keep the group functioning (Scogin and Pollio, 1980; Brooks, 1992).

Many teachers will employ the brain-friendly teaching technique of pausing every twenty minutes in class to have students turn to one another to reflect on the information. I certainly recommend continuing this practice, but have the students first tell each other a joke or story to lighten the moment. If they do not have a joke handy, start one and then have the students fill in the punch line. Humor can fulfill an individual's psychological desire to be part of a group (Scriven and Hefferin, 1998). Moreover, humor creates a bond among students that helps facilitate the accomplishment of tasks (Vinton, 1989, as cited in Scriven and Hefferin, 1998).

Here is a story that has traveled far and wide over the Internet. It probably is not true, but it is interesting and has a point to make.

A philosophy professor stood before his class and had some items in front of him. When class began, wordlessly he picked up a large empty mayonnaise jar and proceeded to fill it with rocks right to the top, rocks about two inches in diameter. He then asked the students if the jar was full. They agreed that it was. The professor then picked up a box of pebbles and poured them into the jar. He shook the jar lightly. The pebbles, of course, rolled into the open areas between the rocks. The students laughed. He asked his students again if the jar was full. They agreed that yes, it was. The professor then picked up a box of sand and poured it into the jar. Of course, the sand filled up everything else. "Now," said the professor, "I want you to recognize that this is your life. The rocks are the important things—your family, your partner, your health, your children—anything that is so important to you that if it were lost, you would be nearly destroyed. The pebbles are the other things in life that matter, but on a smaller scale. The pebbles represent things like your job, your house, your car. The sand is everything else. The small stuff. If you put the sand or the pebbles into the jar first, there is no room for the rocks. The same goes for your life. If you spend all your energy and time on the small stuff, material things, you will never have room for the things that are truly most important. Pay attention to the things that are critical in your life. Play with your children. Take your partner out dancing. There will always be time to go to work, clean the house, give a dinner party and fix the disposal." Take care of the rocks first—the things that really matter. Set your priorities: the rest is just pebbles and sand.

## Practical Examples

You should bring candy or treats to a meeting or class. Give door prizes or candy to individuals for small accomplishments. With a group that does not know you, ask for a volunteer. As you know, people often are afraid of volunteering. Eventually you will get one brave soul to come forward. Simply give him a piece of candy, thank him for volunteering, and let him sit down. The moral of the story is that volunteering may have its rewards, so do not think that it will always be negative. You will be surprised how fast you get a volunteer the next time. For more detailed examples, you may want to check out Sheila Feigelson's book *Energize Your Meetings with Laughter*.

## Action Step 2: Use Humorous Activities within Groups to Build Connectedness

Banning and Nelson (1987) found that humor as a component of an activity will increase group cohesion. If you have students complete group presentations, ask that they incorporate humor. Have students dress up or use props. The funnier or more outrageous the prop, the better. The idea is to have the activity bring people together and influence the social climate of the small group (Duncan, 1982; Duncan, Smeltzer, and Leap, 1990; Duncan and Feisal, 1989; Holmes, 2000). Humor is a great equalizer and it helps new members assimilate into the groups (Brooks, 1992; Duncan and Feisal, 1989). Howard Gardner asserts that there are seven different intelligences, but humor may prove to be number eight—some students who may not test well just might have a great sense of humor.

## Practical Examples

Allow the person taking minutes to integrate clever clip art or jokes. Nobody reads the minutes anyway; at least this way they may look for the jokes. Make people sit by height during the meeting or at tables with people who like soccer, baseball, reading, and so on. Have people engage in activities during a meeting or class: the brain likes it and it can serve a useful purpose. Play games like figuring out brainteasers from a puzzle book, or "wacky-wordy" puzzles. You can find examples on the Internet or in a puzzle magazine (e.g., "now$^{he}$re," which is "he is in the middle of nowhere"). Fun games build cooperation.

## Action Step 3: Have Students Use Games or Mimic *Saturday Night Live* or other Programs

Let's face it, the classroom is not a level playing field. Teachers are in charge and some students are "more equal" than others. Suggesting that students use games like *Jeopardy*, *Who Wants to Be a Millionaire?*, or *The Weakest Link* as part of their presentations helps individuals in a lower-ranking group to "joke back" with higher-status members (Lundberg, 1969; Bradney, 1957). Joking relationships among members of the same status level occur most often, but when joking occurs between status levels, it is typically aimed downward (Brooks, 1992, p. 12). By having students develop games or mimic popular comedy shows, students are shown that joking with the teacher and members of the popular crowd is not only possible but fun. Just as the use of humor by school administrators increases social bonding, which contributes to increased productivity (Ziegler, Boardman, and Thomas, 1985; Williams and Clouse, 1991), the same will hold true for students in class.

## Practical Examples

☺ Laugh with someone and it builds a relationship, but tell a joke to make someone laugh and it builds a power relationship (Pollak and Freda, 1997). As a class activity ask people to tell the most interesting story about themselves. You go first so the group feels comfortable. Without even emphasizing humor, you will get several funny stories. I always tell people that I live in Wisconsin where we save money on clothing because we wear hunting clothes on weekends and then out to formal occasions.

☺ Bring a puzzle to a meeting, class, or event. The more childish the puzzle, the better. In fact, anything having to do with Disney works well. Give everyone approximately five to ten pieces and ask the groups to tell you the subject of the puzzle. Groups typically just look at the pieces to guess the subject, but they should cooperate with other groups to put the pieces together to complete the puzzle. A discussion on teamwork goes a long way.

**5**

# HUMOR IMPROVES COMMUNICATION

There is no higher religion than providing humor to others.

## RESEARCH AND THEORY

**A**ylor, Brooks, Oppliger, and Patrice (2003) examined the use of humor in communication utilizing survey methodology with 188 undergraduate students enrolled in sections of public-speaking courses at a small eastern university. After administering pre- and postsurveys, the researchers used regression analysis and found that humor increases the frequency of out-of-class communication between students and teachers, especially when it comes to informal communication. They also discovered that instructors can promote student satisfaction through the use of humor. The data yielded correlations of 0.35 for instructor humor orientation and out-of-class communication, for an effect size of 0.7 (large). The researchers also found correlations between humor orientation and student satisfaction with out-of-class communication, $r = 0.37$, with an effect size of 0.8 (large).

How school administrators say things is very important. When I first took over an administrator's role in higher education, I was handed three envelopes by the vice president. I was told not to open them until

I ran into trouble. After a short time, I ran into trouble and opened the first envelope, which contained a piece of paper that read, "Open lines of communication." This worked for some time, but again I ran into trouble and had to open the second envelope, whose contents read, "Form a committee." Again, this worked for some time, but I had to open the third envelope after running into trouble a third time. Inside this envelope was a note reading, "Prepare three envelopes."

Having served on various committees throughout my tenure, I have drawn up a list of rules: "Never arrive on time; this stamps you as a beginner. Don't say anything until the meeting is half over; this stamps you as being wise. Be as vague as possible; this avoids irritating the others. When in doubt, suggest that a subcommittee be appointed. Be the first to move for adjournment; this will make you popular; it's what everyone is waiting for." ~ Harry Chapman. And if you don't like these words of wisdom, listen to Mark Twain, who wrote, "Suppose you were an idiot. And suppose you were a member of Congress. But I repeat myself."

## Action Step 1: Humor Is Merely a Tool to Enhance Communication; It Is Not the Answer

Strong communication skills are basic to successful teaching. Crawford (1994b), of the Deptartment of Communication at Fort Hays State University, notes in his research that humor is a communicative tactic used to engender student support. Teachers typically use humor to increase the communication in the classroom, partially through the important symbolic realm to create a positive atmosphere.

Therefore, it is important to be prepared—as with any form of communication. Practice jokes ahead of time and choose your words carefully. For example, be detailed when telling a story. The more details you can add, the more believable it will be. Use the term "ACT scores" instead of "a test." Including dialogue from popular movies is also important to serve as a foundation for a joke, for example, *Caddy Shack*, *Star Wars*, and so forth. Even interesting data can make students pay attention. Robert Putnam wrote in *Bowling Alone*, a great book based on sociological data, that there is a direct correlation between the number of times someone flips the finger and the level of tax evasion. But, of course, "one should use statistics like this as a drunken man uses lampposts—for support rather than for illumination." ~ Andrew Lang.

If the joke works for you, great. If the joke does not work for you, great. Do not give up. When using humor, not everything will work. So what? Deal with it and move on, but do not stop trying. There is no crying in humor. "The analysis of humor, properly conducted, is a delicate dissection of uncertainties, a surgery of suppositions." ~ Stolen from M. J. Moroney.

## Practical Examples

☺ Use stories from *A Cup of Comfort* or *Chicken Soup for the Soul* in class if the verse is related to your material.

☺ Read funny books to the class or allow students to read *Sports Illustrated* or *Dilbert* as assignments.

☺ Look for people to connect with who may have a common experience, or simply steal good ideas from others—this is called research, or plagiarism if you get caught.

☺ You need to get inside the story and feel it; otherwise, people get screen-saver eyes.

☺ Fit the story to the audience.

☺ Write like you speak (www.bradmontgomery.com/general/signature-stories-2/).

☺ Listen to funny CDs on the way to work.

☺ Spend time with humorous people.

☺ Take a break in the day to think about something that makes you laugh (Stephenson and Thibault, 2006, pp. 88–89).

☺ Puns and oxymorons are always appreciated. There are numerous websites dedicated solely to these topics with examples, for example, www.badpuns.com or www.punpunpun.com.

**Table 5.1.   List of oxymorons**

| | | |
|---|---|---|
| 1. Soft rock | 8. Alone together | 15. Military intelligence |
| 2. Sweet sorrow | 9. Passive aggressive | 16. Clearly misunderstood |
| 3. Peace force | 10. Plastic glass | 17. Act naturally |
| 4. Found missing | 11. Good grief | 18. Small crowd |
| 5. Extinct life | 12. Computer security | 19. Definite maybe |
| 6. Exact estimate | 13. Pretty ugly | 20. Working vacation |
| 7. Religious tolerance | 14. Microsoft works | 21. Jumbo shrimp |

## Action Step 2: Use Humor to Achieve Different Levels of Proficiency in Communication

Because the capacity to learn involves psychological factors such as a personality and intelligence, learners achieve different levels of proficiency and overall communicative competence. A review of the literature suggests that the notion of humor competence in second-language learning can be considered the fifth component of the theoretical framework of communicative competence. It involves knowledge of semantic mechanisms of humor, grammar, discourse rules, communication strategies, social norms of language use, and world knowledge. As with the other four competencies (grammatical, sociolinguistic, strategic, and discourse), humor competences contain elements that are transferred from the first language and vary from learner to learner (Vega, 1990).

In other words, knowing and understanding humor can be a distinctive form of communication. Every teacher has read the facts: students remember 10 percent of what they hear, 30 percent of what they see, 50 percent of what they do, and 70 percent of what they teach—or some other similar statistic. (Remember that 98 percent of all statistics are made up. ~ Author unknown.). What is more important is that:

- ☺ Words are 7 percent effective
- ☺ Tone of voice is 38 percent effective
- ☺ Nonverbal cues are 55 percent effective

(I tend to quote a lot of statistics in my work and class, but "statistics are like bikinis. What they reveal is suggestive, but what they conceal is vital." ~Aaron Levenstein). What this means is that you need to paint a picture for the audience through humor using words, pictures, nonverbal cues, body language, and so forth. This can be partially accomplished by three simple concepts: refine, refine, and refine the joke. "Less" is always "more" with a joke. You should set up the joke appropriately, get into the story, tell the punch line, and get out. Moreover, body language is critical. People will be watching your eye movement, body language, and so forth, so you need to make your body work for you when using humor.

## Action Step 3: Humor Is a Form of Communication that Symbolizes the Type of Culture of the Organization

Humor is a trainable skill, a strategy that everyone can use to create a positive environment (Crawford, 1994b). "Humor is useful to leaders who want the ability to symbolize the organization through a non-serious means" (p. 28). In fact, positive uses of humor, such as "developing friendships and being playful, are positively correlated to communication competence" (Graham, Papa, and Brooks, 1992, as cited in Brooks, 1992, p. 11).

### Practical Examples

- ☺ Nonlinguistic representations are not only a recommended teaching tool, but can also be used in funny ways. For example, ask for a show of hands from the audience for those who want the lights turned up brighter. Then, turn the lights up in the room and explain the Chinese proverb, "It just goes to show that more hands make a task lighter."
- ☺ Write down a few pieces of trivia, puns, or pithy sayings and save the information in a PDA file or on your cell phone.
- ☺ Do the alphabet song and "Twinkle, Twinkle, Little Star" have the same tune? Why did you just try singing the two songs above?
- ☺ Put together a sheet of paper with random clip art pieces and ask individuals to select one picture that represents how they are feeling at that moment. You can either use clip art from any software program or go to the wingding font to select an even broader range of pictures. (You may need to enlarge the font size for wingdings.) For example, ✳ ❀ ↙ ✓ ❑.
- ☺ As St. Francis stated, "Preach the gospel always, and if necessary, use words."

## Action Step 4: Let's Be Careful Out There—Appropriate and Inappropriate Forms of Communication and Humor

Pierson and Bredeson (1993) found that elementary school principals who use humor in their daily interactions with teachers seem to enhance their messages and school climate. However, keep your eyes open and don't force the issue. Students will let you know when the humor is appropriate or inappropriate, or when enough is enough (Wanzer et al., 2006).

The following suggestions may help with the concepts on how to apply humor in schools.

1. Verify that the subject matter is appropriate.
2. Identify the target audience and objectives.
3. Use a single unified theme over and over again.
4. Employ positive reinforcement of behavior.
5. Talk with colleagues and students about what is funny (Swanson, 1996).

For example, spend time in the teachers' lounge sharing information. This will give you great ideas while building rapport with colleagues. You should even promote professional-development days on how to use and integrate humor.

## Action Step 5: Cultural Differences of Students Affect the Types of Humor to Be Used

With the realization that the world is flat, teachers need to take into account cultural differences when communicating with staff and students. Humor needs to be used appropriately and with respect for the various cultures in schools today (Prince and Hoppe, 2000). This will take a little extra work. Diversity, and true globalization in the classroom, is fast becoming a reality. If students are not aware of the humor being communicated, they may politely laugh because they think it is the right thing to do. But, Wallinger (1997) notes that "phony or polite laughter as a response to humor should also be a signal to a leader or teacher that an uncomfortable situation exists or that communication is not succeeding" (p. 31). This would be like someone saying, "Oh I get it . . . like humor . . . but different."

## Practical Examples

Bivens et al. (1998) recommend the following (pp. 11–15) practical applications for using humor:

1. Set up humorous literature centers in the classroom.
2. Before putting a book in the literature center, conduct a "book sell" in which a thumbnail sketch is given; use humor in the sell.
3. Read aloud one book by an author who writes humorous literature.
4. Adapt humorous poetry for readers' theater or choral reading.
5. Record humorous selections on tape for children to listen to and read along.
6. Implement humorous literature units for particular types of books: tall tales, humorous poetry, wordplay books, and so on.
7. Engage students in conducting their own research to determine which humorous literature selections have the greatest appeal to children at various grade levels.
8. Use humorous literature as a stimulus for writing activities.
9. Encourage students to tape stories to accompany the illustrations in humorous wordless books.
10. Include examples of regional literature in thematic units.

## Action Step 6: Do Not Hide behind Humor— Use It Appropriately

Humor may actually assist with the uncertainly of communication between cultures.

> Humour's ambiguity enables contentious statements to be made without fear of recrimination. (Remember, Fear is nothing more than False Evidence That Appears Real.) Equally, constructing jokes by juxtaposing two different frames of reference provides a glimpse of alternative (and shared) perceptions of 'reality'. This sensitivity to complexity makes humour a particularly appropriate vehicle for conveying ambitions, subversions, triumphs and failures. (Grugulis, 2002, p. 387)

This concept may be a little like the following story:

> The woman's husband had been slipping in and out of a coma for several months, yet she had stayed by his bedside every single day. One day, when he came to, he motioned for her to come nearer. As she sat by him, he whispered, eyes full of tears, "You know what? You have been with me all

through the bad times. When I got fired, you were there to support me. When my business failed, you were there. When I got shot, you were by my side. When we lost the house, you stayed right here. When my health started failing, you were still by my side. . . . You know what?" "What, dear?" she gently asked, smiling as her heart began to fill with warmth. "I think you're bad luck."

To help with the ambiguity of humor, keep a notebook with you at all times to write down funny comments or observations throughout the day. This needs to become a habit.

## Practical Examples

1. Embrace humor and believe that it works.
2. Know your audience.
3. Begin class with a joke and use humorous stories and anecdotes (Hebert, 1991).

Torok, McMorris, and Lin (2004) examined college students' and teachers' perceptions and identified seven types of humor considered generally positive in the college classroom: funny stories, funny comments, jokes, professional humor, puns, cartoons, and riddles. They also identified types of instructor humor that are perceived negatively: sexual humor, ethnic humor, and aggressive/hostile humor (Wanzer, Frymier, Wojtaszczyk, and Smith, 2006).

## 6

# HUMOR REDUCES
# TENSION AND STRESS

Why does a round pizza come in a square box?

**D**an Goleman, noted expert on emotional intelligence, writes that we can easily change the mood of the people around us through emotional responses. Of course, most of us are willing to change not because we see the light, but because we feel the heat. Teachers who laugh have the ability to transform a classroom into a positive place. Laughter starts out as an internal process that soon becomes a social function. How does this happen, and how can it relieve stress in a person or group?

## STRESS

Real stress is when your boss says to you, "I like you. You remind me of myself when I was young and stupid." When stress strikes, hormones called cortisol and epinephrine together raise a person's blood pressure and circulating blood sugar level. Cortisol lowers the effectiveness of the immune system. There are several stages to stress that can ultimately lead to physical, as well as emotional, ailments. It is interesting to note that science indicates that laughter lowers serum cortisol levels in the

body and improves the body's disease-fighting capabilities while relieving stress (Martin and Dobbin, 1985).

Research also tells us that when a person laughs and is joyful, the
body releases endorphins, the brain's natural painkillers, into the body.
"The connection between stress and high blood pressure, muscle tension, immunosuppression, and many other changes has been known for
years. We now have evidence that laughter creates the opposite effects.
It appears to be the perfect antidote for stress" (Wooten, 1996, p. 2).

## RESEARCH AND THEORY

Kuiper, Grimshaw, Leite, and Kirsh (2004) conducted an experiment
at the University of Western Ontario with 137 college students, using
various measures of humor. The results indicate the following correlations:

- Affiliative humor with coping humor, $r = 0.49$—1.15 effect size
- Self-enhancing humor with coping humor, $r = 0.60$—1.5 effect
  size
- Skilled humor with rude humor, $r = 0.50$—1.15 effect size
- Skilled humor with coping humor, $r = 0.49$—1.15 effect size
- Social self-esteem with coping humor scale, $r = 0.37$—0.8 effect
  size

The main conclusion was that the use of certain forms of humor is
correlated significantly to lower levels of anxiety and depression, $r = -0.28$, $-0.32$, respectively, and effect sizes of 0.55 and 0.65.

### Action Step 1: Stress Is Part of Almost Every Classroom, and the Use of Humor, Laughter, and a Positive Environment in the Classroom Should Help Decrease the Levels of Stress

Stress is part of the classroom environment. Instructors have the stress
of collecting and presenting the material, and students have the stress of
studying and understanding the material and taking tests to demonstrate
that understanding" (Edwards and Gibboney, 1992, p. 2). When individu-

als are anxious, the body releases stress hormones. These stress hormones suppress the immune system, putting individuals more at risk for illness. As noted previously, laughter may have the opposite effect of stress.

A wide range of low-risk humor techniques can be very effective in reducing anxiety and improving learning and performance. However, teaching almost always involves students, so my advice is that if you have a lot of tension and you get a headache from teaching, do what it says on the aspirin bottle: "Take two aspirin" and "Keep away from children." ~ Author unknown.

## Practical Examples

☺   Funny handouts never get boring. You can certainly use cartoons (being careful of copyright issues), historical sayings, or even clip art. The idea is to mix it up—do something different from just the traditional handouts.

☺   Start or end class with a knock knock joke. You can find a new joke online each day.

> Knock knock.
> Who's there?
> Interrupting cow.
> Interrupting cow wh . . . Moo!!!!

☺   Lists are an excellent way of combining humor with content. David Letterman is the king of top ten lists, but that does not preclude others from using the concept. Allow students to solve a problem or brainstorm new ideas with humorous solutions. The humorous lists will not only help release tension, they may also lead to unconventional solutions. You might make a humorous list by copying David Letterman and just changing a few items to match your material or by having a normal list of items for students to do with two or three silly ones added in.

Example of Top Ten List: World's Thinnest Books

1. *Things I Can't Afford* by Bill Gates
2. *Things I Would Not Do for Money* by Dennis Rodman

3. *The Wild Years* by Al Gore
4. *Amelia Earhart's Guide to the Pacific Ocean*
5. *America's Most Respected Lawyers*
6. *Dr. Kevorkian's Collection of Motivational Speeches*
7. *Everything Men Know about Women*
8. *Spotted Owl Recipes* by The Sierra Club
9. The Amish Phone Directory
10. *My Book of Morals* by Bill Clinton and Gary Condit (with a fore-word by the Reverend Jesse Jackson)

## Action Step 2: As the Teacher, You Need to Model Humor

Smith and Powell (1988) concluded that individuals using self-disparaging humor are perceived as more effective at relieving tension and even summarizing the opinions of group members. If you want students to enjoy learning, you need to enjoy teaching. Have fun in class. Make fun of yourself and tell jokes; the students will follow suit. I happen to be a die-hard Green Bay Packers fan and sit with a small Packers doll next to me as I watch football. I am sure that this doll is responsible for every Packers victory, and therefore, I take the credit for every Green Bay Packers victory. You would be surprised how many students talk of similar superstitions after I tell this story.

### Practical Examples

Overhead transparencies are a necessity for any teacher. There are some standard transparencies that you may want to carry with you. An assortment of jokes from cartoons like *Dilbert* are not only practical but funny. Pithy sayings will also go a long way to make your point, and when you have them on a transparency ready to go, it makes a lasting impression. Here are some examples:

- ☺ Don't sweat the small stuff; everything is the small stuff.
- ☺ "If you command wisely, you will be obeyed cheerfully." ~ Thomas Fuller.
- ☺ If you dig yourself into a hole, then the least you can do is stop digging for a minute.

☺ It is good to get into hot water because at least it keeps you clean.

☺ There are three kinds of people in the world today:

1. Those who make things happen
2. Those who watch things happen
3. Those who wonder what happened

Activities can be interesting, humorous, and informative. Learn three or four activities that you can do at the drop of a hat. Leaders can use the activities for any of the purposes listed in this chapter. One such activity is juggling. This is actually easier than you may think. Simply read any number of books on how to juggle. With a little practice you can demonstrate juggling to a group while making numerous analogies. For example, learning to juggle can be associated with juggling projects at school or the ideas that practice makes perfect, hard work can make things happen, or learning transpires best when theory and practice are integrated. Another activity could be card tricks. Once again, a good book on card tricks can make you a magician within minutes. Card tricks can also have many metaphors associated with them, such as communication, people's deceiving activities, teachers' sleight of hand, or making order out of chaos. All it takes is a little hard work. But of course, remember that hard work pays off in the future while laziness pays off now.

### Action Step 3: Use Jokes to Reduce Student Anxiety and to Defuse Stressful Situations

Every day in every class, something happens that teachers do not expect. Students misbehave, an argument breaks out, students complain about one another, students do not do their homework, and so forth. According to Morreall (1983), "humor is created by a reduction of anxiety or relaxation of strain. Winnick (1976) argues that jokes can defuse tension in the form of conflict mediation, 'Humor is one way of bringing problems back to a manageable size'" (Crawford, 1994b, p. 12). Humor helps break conflict and boredom, and reduces tension and fatigue and helps people relax (Hurren, 2001; Hudson, 1979; Meyer, 1990; Morreall, 1983). "Humor can be used to distance unpleasant, stressful, or boring parts of our lives by allowing us to regard them with less seriousness" (Brooks, 1992, p. 11).

If you, as the teacher, react to stress with more stress, students will follow your lead. However, if you react to stress with humor, students will also follow your lead. Keep a few jokes handy on a sheet of paper, in your head, or on the computer, and use them when you need to divert attention from a stressful situation. Dalton A. Kehoe, an associate professor of communication studies at York University, notes that he actually stops his class every fifteen minutes for a three-minute comedy break during which he shows a humorous video clip. Kehoe makes a contest out of the break by allowing students to submit their favorite videos from YouTube and elsewhere. Students look forward to the break from the lecture and the stress of school (Young, chronicle.com/free/v54/i41/41a00901.htm).

## Practical Examples

- ☺ We can listen four times faster than people can speak, so we tend to take "field trips" when someone is talking. Follow the example of Dalton Kehoe with video interludes.
- ☺ "Conflict in itself is not a bad thing. What's important is the way in which we deal with conflict." ~ Bishop Frey.
- ☺ Playing games like *Jeopardy* is a favorite technique of many teachers and certainly promotes funny responses, even without trying.
- ☺ As a teacher or administrator, take care of the little things. Even funny screen savers on your computer promote humor.
- ☺ Invite students to participate in the creation of a school song, motto, or logo.
- ☺ Hold assemblies, present funny awards, and allow students to be creative in building school spirit.
- ☺ Organize a student talent show to celebrate the end of a term or school year.
- ☺ Invite motivational speakers or comedy troupes to make presentations for teachers and students, but be sure to connect

the comedy to class material (Stephenson and Thibault, 2006, p. 91).

## Action Step 4: Use Humor on Tests, Homework, Your Syllabus, and Notes to Parents

Grades, tests, and homework are all areas that can create stress for students, so why not liven them up with some well-placed jokes? Humor can moderate or even alleviate the negative effect of stress directly (Humphreys, 1990, p. 30). Tests don't have to be completely serious—put in jokes or funny cartoons.

### Practical Examples

☺ It is no secret that students need variety in the classroom. The days of "lecture and lose 'em" are gone. Teachers need to use a variety of teaching styles and different visuals. In other words, the more cartoons, sayings, games, short videos, pictures, and so on you are able to use in class, the better you will be at generating interest; students appreciate humor and consequently will take a greater interest in class.

☺ Here are a few more guidelines:

 1. Use a modicum of apt, relevant humor in an informative presentation.
 2. Self-disparaging humor enhances the presenter's image.
 3. Humor is only one factor that enhances interest.
 4. Apt, relevant humor does not affect persuasiveness.
 5. Satire has unpredictable results (Zemke, 1991).

☺ Do not try to please everyone in the group. Alfie Kohn writes that you cannot motivate others because internal motivation is more powerful than extrinsic motivation. As a leader/teacher, you should use humor to simply provide the atmosphere conducive to learning.

☺ Remember, it is frustrating when you know all the answers, but nobody bothers to ask you the questions. Laugh at yourself and you will always be amused.

## Action Step 5: Humor Is Healthy

"Laughter, along with an active sense of humor, may help protect you against a heart attack," according to a study by cardiologists at the University of Maryland Medical Center in Baltimore (University of Maryland, 2000, p. 1). Researchers compared humor responses in three hundred people: half the participants had either suffered a heart attack or had undergone coronary artery bypass surgery, while the other half were healthy. The researchers found that the healthy group laughed more.

Many researchers actually compare humor's biological impact on the human body to that of physical exercise. Exercise enhances one's sense of well-being; humor and laughter improve one's outlook on life (Wallinger, 1997; see also Sleeter, 1981; Weinstein, 1986; Crawford, 1994b; Swift and Swift, 1994). Cogan, Cogan, Waltz, and McCue (1987) conducted several experiments and found that laughter allegedly had pain-reducing effects (Humphreys, 1990, p. 35).

## Practical Examples—the Use of Stories

Howard Gardner (1996) writes that "the right anecdote [story] can be worth a thousand theories," but it uses up a thousand times more memory. Students appreciate stories and typically pay attention because they are eager to hear the ending. Real-life stories actually work better than fictitious ones. Make them short and sweet with one main point. You need to listen to what students say in class so you know what types of stories may work best. Remember that light travels faster than sound. That is why some people appear bright until you hear them speak.

I have three kids, and you know how it is with kids. With the first one we bought one of those toys where you put round pegs in round holes. As soon as Katie put the first peg in, we got out the video camera and called the newspapers and TV stations. When our second child, Mel, figured out that the round peg goes into the round hole as I was walking by her one day, I said, "Hey, Nancy, look what Mel did." When our third child was in middle school, I said to my wife, "Hey, did we ever buy Kevin one of those toys with the round pegs and round holes?"

Stories work wonders to make your point.

## Action Step 6: Teachers Are More Energetic When They Use Humor

"If humor reduces stress, increases creativity, and boosts energy . . . it seems reasonable to think it would have similar benefits in the classroom. It would be expected that instructors who perform better and are energetic would be evaluated more favorably by students. It also seems reasonable to think that the reduction of stress and the increase in creativity would facilitate student learning" (Edwards and Gibboney 1992, p. 3). Teachers and students who use humor are better prepared to handle the stress of trusting another individual. This is due to the way a good-humored individual perceives stress. By finding humor in a stressful situation, one can adapt better to the situation (Hampes, 2001).

There are many students (and teachers) who can "go off" at even the slightest provocation. Humor can serve to reduce these flare-ups (Rareshide, 1993, p. 18) and "can also be used as a coping mechanism for managing anxiety and embarrassment by diverting attention from the situation that caused the embarrassment" (Fink and Walker, 1977; Ziv, 1984, 1988; as cited in Brooks, 1992, p. 11).

### Practical Examples

☺ Have students do some role-playing in class. Nothing elaborate—students can even stay in their own seats to take on the role of the person being discussed in class. You are not looking for perfect responses, but rather for students to place themselves in the moment and use some critical-thinking skills.

☺ Rap songs may not be your niche, but students should be able to integrate them into assignments, and if you try one (or two) in class, you will be an instant hit. The president of our university used a rap in her annual state of the university address. This is typically a serious occasion, and the rap made it much more interesting and memorable.

☺ A close relative of rap songs is the funny chant, and these chants can serve as a mnemonic device when learning new material. You may want to develop one spontaneously if the class is starting to get out of control.

☺ Take students on exciting and fun field trips—sometimes the more out of the norm, the better (Stephenson and Thibault, 2006, p. 66).

☺ Make story problems funny. For example, instead of saying, "If a train is traveling ten miles per hour," and so on, go with "If *Battlestar Galactica* is traveling four times the speed of sound and hits a black hole," and so on.

☺ Pose a series of questions to students about the nature of humor and discuss their answers either as a whole class or in small groups (Stephenson and Thibault, 2006, p. 70).

## Action Step 7: Humor as a Healing Tool

As you know, there are small concerns in the world, and there are much larger concerns. After the 9/11 attacks many Americans, especially the young, looked for ways to heal. Some found it in humor. A story beginning on the front page of the March 19, 2002, *Washington Post* looks at how local teenagers are using new terrorism slang from the event of 9/11 to ease tension. The author, Emily Wax, writes, "Messy bedrooms are 'ground zero.' A petty concern is 'so September 10.' The word 'hottie,' once used to describe an attractive teenage male, has been replaced by 'firefighter cute'" (Binderman, 2002).

## Practical Examples

☺ Use books to assist you. Obviously, this particular book is the best, but another option is Diane Hodges's *Laugh Lines for Educators*, which is filled with numerous examples of jokes and stories that work well in the classroom. The examples range from elementary-school-aged students to high school. Also look into Richard Shade's *License to Laugh: Humor in the Classroom* or Ronald Berk's *Professors Are from Mars, Students Are from Snickers*; both books contain excellent examples.

☺ Listed below is an interesting and humorous paragraph. Have students read the information and then discuss it. Why are they able to read the material? (Just another example of humor found in "junk mail" sent to me—and a few million others.)

Subject: Typogylcemia

I cdnuolt blveiee taht I cluod aulaclty uesdnatnrd waht I was rdanieg. The phaonmneal pweor of the hmuan mnid. Aoccdrnig to a rscheearch at Cmabrigde Uinervtisy, it deosn't mttaer in waht oredr the ltteers in a wrod are, the olny iprmoatnt tihng is taht the frist and lsat ltteer be in the rghit pclae. The rset can be a taotl mses and you can sitll raed it wouthit a porbelm. Tihs is bcuseae the huamn mnid deos not raed ervey lteter by istlef, but the wrod as a wlohe. Amzanig huh? Yaeh and I awlyas thought slpeling was ipmorantt.

# 7

# HUMOR PROMOTES CREATIVITY AND DIVERGENT THINKING

Teaching with humor is doing a common thing, uncommonly well.

In a study of personnel directors at 100 of the nation's largest corporations, 84 percent of the subjects reported that people with a sense of humor are more creative, less rigid, and more willing to try new ideas (Philbrick 1991). They say (although I am not sure who "they" are) that information doubles every six months. If this is correct, by the time you finish your freshman year of college you will be two years behind the flow of knowledge—not exactly a good investment for your $100,000 in tuition. You'd better have a good sense of humor to deal with all this. A keen sense of humor is what makes people more creative and more innovative, and ultimately assists them in the job market, that is, being entrepreneurial. They (here we go again with "they") say that a strong liberal arts education really assists individuals to be well-rounded thinkers, learners, writers, readers, and so on. Of course, not everyone appreciates creativity. After all, it just may be easier to change the location of a cemetery than to change the thinking of some school administrators.

Here is an example of creativity. An English professor wrote the words "a woman without her man is nothing" on the blackboard and directed the students to punctuate it correctly. The men wrote: "A woman, without her man, is nothing." The women wrote: "A woman: without her, man is nothing."

## RESEARCH AND THEORY

In 1972, Hauck and Thomas conducted a study of three random groups of eighty elementary school students and found correlations between intelligence, creativity, and humor. For example, sense of humor correlated highly with both creativity, $r = 0.89$, and intelligence, $r = 0.91$. These results should come as no surprise to educators. Students who are creative tend to be funny, and also tend to be the more successful students in school. (What does the successful liberal arts major say to the business major? "Do you want fries with that order?")

### Action Step 1: Humor and Critical Thinking

Stand-up comics tell you that so long as we have politicians, we will never run out of jokes. For example,

A city boy, Andy, moved to the country and bought a donkey from an old farmer for $100. The farmer agreed to deliver the donkey the next day. The next day, the farmer drove up and said, "Sorry, but I have some bad news. The donkey died." "Well, then, just give me my money back."

"Can't do that. I went and spent it already."

"OK, then. Just unload the donkey."

"What ya gonna do with him?"

"I'm going to raffle him off."

"You can't raffle off a dead donkey!"

"Sure I can. Watch me. I just won't tell anybody he's dead."

A month later the farmer met up with the city boy and asked, "What happened with that dead donkey?"

"I raffled him off. I sold five hundred tickets at two dollars apiece and made a profit of $898."

"Didn't anyone complain?"

"Just the guy who won. So I gave him his two dollars back!"

This boy grew up to be a politician.

Teachers have known for some time that practical applications of material are important in the learning process. Using real and humorous observations can prove to be just as important. For example, Humke and Schaefer (1996) studied eighty-six adults (all Caucasians) from urban and middle-class backgrounds. They found a strong correlation between the creativity scores and the humor scores. People are creative, so they can be funny. Teachers simply need to develop humor along with their natural observations. One successful technique is to use similes, comparisons, and contrasts with real-life observations. For example, contrasting two incongruent ideas is almost always funny. Use practical examples, like explaining that a successful Democratic president is probably the most incongruent idea around (just kidding).

## Practical Examples

☺ Teachers can serve as models of humor within their direct instructional role.
   1. Tell or read stories with incongruous actions, language, settings, or characters.
   2. Use exaggerated speech or facial expressions.
   3. Direct and participate in learning-related games that give risk-free practice.
☺ Indirect facilitation can be accomplished by selecting learning materials such as tapes, books, or movies of silly songs and stories that foster opportunities for informal interactions (Gentile and McMillan, 1987, pp. 4–8).

This is not a new concept; even Aristotle in book 3 of *Rhetoric* advocates using humor to destroy an opponent's argument. In today's world, there is a generic process on how to develop your own humor for teaching.

1. Brainstorm the main topic area that you need to discuss.
2. Brainstorm ideas and facts about the topic—allow humorous examples to come forward.
3. Write observations on the facts.

4. It is easier to write jokes about the real-life observations you have experienced.

Ziv (1984) may have said it best when he theorized that "humor serves to provide a sense of momentary freedom by twisting the usual rules of logical thinking" (Brooks, 1992, p. 17). There is a certain mental flexibility associated with humor that eventually leads to innovative ideas (Brooks, 1992, p. 17).

- ☺ Use puzzles and brainteasers in class, for example, from *Game* magazine.
- ☺ Discuss political cartoons and have students give humorous analogies.
- ☺ Use impromptu reenactments of history, for example, the Battle of Marathon; again, the more complex, the better (Brooks, 1991; Graham, Papa, and Brooks, 1992). A colleague, Mike Dickmann, has students discuss how the history of America would have been different if the first colonists had settled in California and not New England.
- ☺ Have younger students research their families' funny personal stories.
- ☺ Investigate humor in local or national news.

## Action Step 2: Humor Can Enhance Student Interest, but Teachers Need to "Read" the Class for Reactions and Acceptance

Humor certainly can be used as a pedagogical tool that enhances the interest of students and provides a means to engage in divergent thinking (Dodge and Rossett, 1982). Nevertheless, you need to be cognizant of your students. Listen to what they are saying and watch how they are reacting to your humor and the lessons—read their mannerisms. Good humor is one thing, but students still need to be able to take notes on the material, no matter how funny it may be. Formative feedback is essential in the classroom, but you can also have fun with assessment. I suggest giving ten large cards with 1 to 10 written on them to three or four students in class. Instruct them to hold up the cards rating the jokes and the material presented in class. When you receive tens, compare yourself to Nadia Comaneci, and if you receive lower scores, you can joke about how you stole that joke from a colleague you don't like anyway. Or, you can simply ask students to give you a thumbs-up (for good), thumbs-down (for bad), or thumbs-sideways (for do not know), but be sure to use the thumb and not other fingers in this activity. Ask students for their suggestions on how to provide formative feedback, emphasizing creativity and humor in their responses.

## Practical Examples

☺ Thinking creatively: allow students to use humor to be more innovative. For example, bring in prompts that are innovative to help students and staff. Use a picture of a camera to tell people to "stay focused" or of orange juice to "concentrate."

☺ Remember, you do not always want creativity; for example, creative drivers on the highway are not cool.

## Action Step 3: Humor Drives Dendrites, Works the Brain, and Improves Thinking

"When people are laughing, their brains seem to operate more efficiently and symmetrically. Humor seems to facilitate a more balanced cerebral activity that leads to creative thinking. This creative thinking produces different solutions to problems than the individual or group might otherwise generate" (Scriven and Hefferin, 1998, p. 14).

The main function of the brain is to keep you alive by storing information vital to survival and getting rid of information that has no effect on this goal. Interestingly, the brain weighs approximately three pounds and uses ten times more oxygen than your lungs; this is 25 percent of all energy produced by the body. Your brain really works, automatically storing survival information in one of several different types of memory. The key is to get your brain to store the necessary information that will enhance learning. The brain is comprised of neurons (brain cells) with dendrites (tentacles of communication) that send impulses through synapses (gaps between dendrites) using chemical reactions.

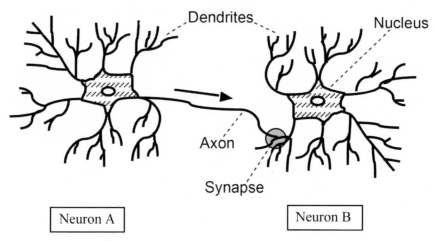

**Figure 7.1. Dendrites and neurons**

The brain is a complex organ, so in order to assist the learning process, the more connections that can be made to previous knowledge, the more efficient the learning process. Consequently, through occurrences that happen every day, the synapses in the brain make the connections through the mistakes you make over time and the learning that takes place. Speaking of mistakes, I remind students that the sooner you fall behind the more time you have to catch up.

All sensory input passes through the amygdala, which is the security part of the brain that determines emotional responses. It is the survival part of the brain, and it constantly asks the question, do I eat it, does it eat me, or do I mate with it? The brain needs to understand the content of the information to be learned, it must be deemed important, and then it has to be connected to some other relevant information already stored in memory. (Of course, a clear conscience is usually the sign of a bad memory.) Because humor is a universal language, the concept is already stored in the working memory of most people, so learning activities tied to humor can be connected in the brain more readily and thereby more easily stored in memory.

Research also informs us that humor is more a consequence of nurture than of nature, but the latter certainly plays a role.

Once upon a time, there were a frog and a scorpion. The scorpion approached the frog and asked for a ride on his back across a pond. The frog said, "No, because you will sting me and we will drown." The scorpion responded, "No, I won't because I need you. I have to get across the pond and cannot swim. It would do me no good to sting you. Because we both would drown if I did that." The frog agreed and was taking the scorpion across the pond when in the middle of the journey the scorpion stung the frog. As the two of them were sinking to certain death, the frog asked, "Why did you do that?" The scorpion responded, "I'm a scorpion and it's just my nature."

The brain can certainly learn new material, but it would rather connect to it through previous information because this makes the work of the neurons, dendrites, and synapses operate more efficiently. Nevertheless, it is interesting to note that people actually remember less than 1 percent of what they see, hear, feel, smell, and taste every day (this should help explain some of those low grades in high school). Through the five senses of the body, the information goes to the area of the brain called the *sensory register*, or the *reticular activation system* (RAS), located in the brain stem. Through a process of filtering, pertinent information for survival goes into short-term memory and/or working memory. At any time, if the brain decides that the information is useless (like reality TV shows), it is not stored or processed further. If the brain can make a connection to previous experiences, or make sense out of the information, and if it fits into the cognitive belief system, then it may be stored in the long-term memory, that is, we learn it. However, survival and emotional data have priority over cognitive processing. The amygdala is always filtering information to see if it should raise an emotion out of the body or if it is a danger to the brain and body (again, reality TV fits into this category). David Sousa notes that the brain is a "lean, mean pattern-making machine." With more than forty thousand bits of information going into the brain every second, the brain must decide quickly and accurately what needs to be remembered and why. The brain does not really like details—it would rather look for trends or the "gist" of the material. This information corresponds to Benjamin Bloom's taxonomy of knowledge, with memorization of details on the lower end of the scale of learning and evaluation on the higher end with the assessment of patterns as we look at the bigger picture. For the brain to make patterns, it needs to make connections with previous information learned, and the material must be relevant. The bottom line is that people know and appreciate humor. If you connect learning to something funny, students remember the funny component and connect it to the new concept, and will learn it.

Von Oech (1990) suggests that humor (a) stretches thinking, which helps develop alternative ideas, (b) promotes ambiguity and the unusual combinations of ideas, and (c) allows conventional rules to be challenged. Von Oech states that "there is a close relationship between the 'haha' of humor and the 'ahah' of discovery" (p. 93). For example, I am sure you received the e-mail that was being sent around with the pictures and associated creative titles. You may have deleted this e-mail. I saved it and use it all the time in class to have students work on their critical-thinking skills, and then I show them the answers. Post each picture for students to see and ask them to simply explain what the picture is. Students' creativity should take over as they attempt to guess the following captions.

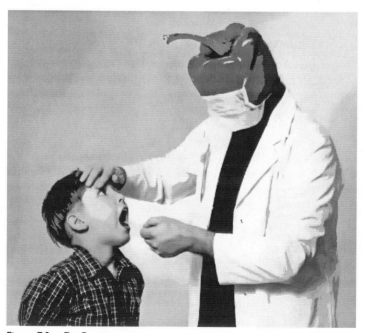

Figure 7.2.   Dr. Pepper

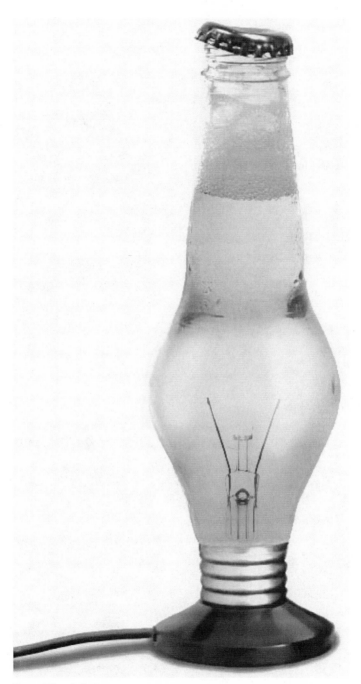

Figure 7.3.  Light beer

Figure 7.4.   Egg plant

Figure 7.5.   Card shark

Figure 7.6.   Pool table

Figure 7.7.    iPod

Figure 7.8.    Assaulted peanut

Figure 7.9. Gator aid

## Practical Examples

☺ Combine humor and a modified Delphi system. Have individuals respond to a question, problem, or situation by writing responses on butcher paper. Then, give colored dots to everyone. You can buy different kinds of dots, like ones with pictures on them, or you can make your own with a computer. Each person gets three dots and can place them on any solution he or she wants. You can put all three on one item or divide up your dots. This activity not only gets people up and walking around, but talking as well. The Delphi process can take many different avenues at this point, but usually you take the top five items and repeat the process until you get down to one. Allow students to be creative and funny in their responses—the two actually go hand-in-hand.

☺ If you make a mistake or mess, a quote from Dr. Seuss can be very profound:

> But your mother will come,
> She will find this big mess!
> And this mess is so big
> And so deep and so tall,
> We cannot pick it up.
> There is no way at all!

☺ Divide your class into groups of three to five participants. Hold up several ordinary objects, such as a pen, chalk, glasses, and so on. Make the groups find the most original, the most useless, and the funniest use for each of the objects. The idea is to have fun with the exercise while promoting teamwork and creativity.

☺ Have students come up with new and cool things to do in school. For example:

Cool Things to Do

1. Page yourself over the intercom and do not disguise your voice.
2. Put your garbage can on your desk and label it "In."
3. As often as you can, skip rather than walk.

Or ask your students "interesting" questions:

1. Why do we say something is out of whack? What is "whack"?
2. When someone asks you for "a penny for your thoughts" and "you put your two cents in," what happens to the other penny?
3. Why are a wise man and a wise guy opposite?
4. Do people read the Bible more as they get older because they are cramming for the final exam?

5. If it is true that we are here to help others, then what exactly are the others here for?

## Action Step 4: Humor Can Help with Creative Problem Solving

Small-group decision making and creative problem solving are some of the most important activities that groups undertake. Laughter may not help you to escape problems, but teachers can use it to improve their ability to handle problems in a calm and efficient manner. At Cornell University, researchers found that students are more creative when humor is used in the classroom. Students who watched funny films had greater success solving problems. It may be that humor helps the mind switch from its usual patterns of logic to more creative patterns (Brooks, 1992, p. 15; see also Edwards and Gibboney, 1992; Poole, 1985).

### Practical Examples

*Six Hats*    In the early 1980s, Dr. de Bono invented the Six Thinking Hats method. The method is a framework for thinking and can incorporate lateral thinking. Valuable judgmental thinking has its place in the system but is not allowed to dominate as in normal thinking. There are six metaphorical hats and the thinker can put on or take off one of these hats to indicate the type of thinking being used. This putting on and taking off is essential. The hats must never be used to categorize individuals, even though their behavior may seem to invite this. When this method is done in groups, everybody wears the same hat at the same time (de Bono, 1985, as cited in members.optusnet.com.au/~charles57/Creative/Techniques/sixhats.htm).

Not to tinker with a classic, but adding a seventh hat, humor, would enhance the creative thinking process. By the way, the hat should be plaid, to go along with de Bono's white, red, black, yellow, green, and blue ones.

In *License to Laugh*, Richard Shade offers some ideas on how to use humor in the classroom in creative ways.

1. Rewrite fairy tales, myths, or stories. Make them fun, funny, and creative.

2. Photograph candid shots of students during various school activities and ask other students to provide captions for each picture.
3. Have a "backward" day in class where you reverse the day's order, read from back to front, or maybe even put clothes on backward.
4. Integrate humor into routine internal correspondence. Use quotes, cartoons, or funny expressions.
5. Write your own humorous lyrics to favorite songs, much like "Weird Al" Yankovic. Try to connect the songs to the material in class.
6. Have students create "Tom Swifties," phrases that use double meanings. For example,
   a. "Get to the point," he said sharply.
   b. "These hot dogs are really good," she said frankly.
7. Allow students to design and send humorous birthday cards or holiday cards to members of the class (pp. 66–68).

## Action Step 5: Humor Can Help with Creative Decision Making

Scholars recognize that there are two main types of tasks for groups: decision making and creative problem solving (Miner, 1979). As noted previously, one benefit of humor is to enhance relationships and build teamwork. Moreover, it can stretch students' minds for creative decision making.

Even de Bono thinks that lateral thinking is closely related to insight, creativity, and humor (de Bono, 1970, p. 9). Part of this may be explained by the fact that "with the reduction of stress through laughter, there is more time and energy left to learn and create. The instructor and students feel a freedom that encourages divergent thinking and creativity" (Walters, 1995, p. 44). Humor is highly correlated with insight (Allport, 1961); moreover, laughter counteracts stress, and "increases energy and creativity" (Edwards and Gibboney, 1992, p. 24). De Bono believes that humor may be one of the most significant behaviors of the human brain partially because it indicates better than any other mental behavior the nature of the information system that gives rise to perception. Humor not only clearly indicates the nature of the system but also shows how perceptions set up in one way can suddenly be reconfigured in another way. This is the essence of creativity.

## Practical Examples

☺ Use props, toys, and technology. In fact, technology software games are wonderful learning tools. Hollywood High is just one example of software developed by educational specialists that allows students to make their own interactive cartoons. With this software, you write, direct, and produce the stories that are made into animations, which can then be connected to class material.

☺ Let students adopt a favorite TV program to discuss at the start of class. Ask them to be creative relating material from class to the show.

☺ Have students develop a Humor Improvement Plan (HIP) for themselves, for example, how they will use humor.

Here is an example of higher-order, and creative, thinking through humor. The jokes cover similar topics, but the third one actually makes students think more critically because it requires more background knowledge.

1. A sandwich goes into a bar and the bartender says, "You can't come in here, we don't serve sandwiches."
2. A grasshopper walks into a bar. The bartender says, "Hey, we have a drink named after you." The grasshopper responds, "Wow, that's great. You have a drink named Peter?"
3. A dyslexic walks into a bra.

# 8

## HUMOR CAN HELP
## ADJUST STUDENT BEHAVIOR

If you can't be kind, at least have the decency to be vague.

—Anonymous

Laughter not only helps to release negative emotions, like anger that has been stored up in the body (Stephenson and Thibault, 2006, p. 10), but it can also produce social pressure among students to conform to norms, reinforce group norms, and build emotional intelligence. Laughter can provide a cathartic release, a purifying of emotions and release of emotional tension. Laughter, crying, raging, and trembling are all cathartic activities that can unblock energy flow. However, one of the most important benefits of humor may be that it can engage students in learning. An engaged student is typically a well-behaved student who is learning. Speaking of being well behaved, it is interesting to note that in prison, you get time off for good behavior, but as a teacher, you get rewarded for good behavior with more work.

### RESEARCH AND THEORY

The research on student engagement may be just as diverse as the findings on humor. Several meta-analyses found three main forms of engagement: emotional, behavioral, and cognitive (Fredericks, Blumenfeld, and Paris, 2004). It appears that humor may have a positive influence on all three forms of engagement. It has been found that engagement is responsive to variations in the environment and can point to specific school and classroom changes. In other words, the introduction of humor into the classroom could have a direct effect on student engagement, thereby improving the learning environment. But, change takes time. Remember, "We are not where we want to be. . . . We are not where we are going to be. . . . But, we are not where we were." ~ Rosa Parks.

Duay (2007), Fry and Allen (2004), Hurren (2001), Coleman (1992), Pedde (1996), and Crawford (1994b) all write that humor in schools helps to facilitate motivation, holds the attention of children, and increases the engagement of students. All these researchers concluded that teachers use humor in a variety of ways to increase engagement. Remember, children will not care what you know unless they know that you care.

## Action Step 1: Use Humor to Express Approval and Disapproval of Behavior in the Classroom

"As a means of social control, humor may function as a control mechanism to express approval or disapproval of actions, especially disapproval of violations of group norms" (Brooks, 1992, p. 11). Any verbal or nonverbal communication, such as eye contact, gestures, words, and so forth, can be humorous in nature and send a message to the student about his or her behavior (ASCD, 2001, p. 3). As the teacher, you can not only control behavior, but also reinforce group norms by using humor to make an example of the student (Stephenson, 1951; Brooks, 1992, p. 11). Provine writes that if a student abruptly leaves class in the middle, the teacher might call out, "Men's room is down the hall to the left," thereby showing his concern for the student's action without being confrontational. Sometimes, self-disparaging humor can be used to control situations much like the humor used to put down others (Crawford, 1994b, p. 14). Or, if a student is creating a disturbance in class, say something like, "Remember, every time I speak I must ask myself if I am improving on the silence," an example used previously.

## Practical Examples

☺ Eliminate the problem of class clowns and associated negative behavior by electing your own "classroom jester" for the week. This student will be given the responsibility of sharing humor in various fashions throughout the day, or you can have the "classroom jester" use a ten-point scale to evaluate the humor of students. In this way, when the class clown acts up, the classroom jester negates the response by rating the humor and taking away negative effects (Shade, 1996, p. 69).

☺ Humor can make life more productive and tolerable. Use jokes when things are going well and also when they are not going so well in the classroom. Just as in sports, never get too high with the victories or too low with the defeats.

☺ Keep a book of jokes or cartoons handy and read from it, especially if the class starts getting out of control. Just pull out the book and start reading jokes. You will be amazed at how students stop what they are doing and pay attention. This is one of the few times when jokes do not have to be tied directly to the material because you are more concerned about behavior than learning at this point.

1. How do you catch a unique rabbit? Unique up on it.
2. How do you catch a tame rabbit? Tame way.
3. What do fish say when they hit a concrete wall? Dam!
4. What do you call a boomerang that doesn't work? A stick.
5. What do you call cheese that isn't yours? Nacho cheese.
6. What do you call Santa's helpers? Subordinate Clauses.
7. What do you call four bullfighters in quicksand? Quattro sinko.
8. What do you get from a pampered cow? Spoiled milk.
9. What do you get when you cross a snowman with a vampire? Frostbite.
10. What's the difference between a bad golfer and a bad skydiver? A bad golfer goes, "Whack, dang!" A bad skydiver goes, "Dang! Whack."

☺ Do not be afraid to use humor when reinforcing positive aspects of students. The teacher's job of recognizing students is never done. For example, while traveling through a small town in the South a visitor saw an old man sitting on the porch of his house. He asked the man if he had lived here his whole life and the man replied, "Not yet."

☺ Utilize analogies that transform abstract ideas into more familiar examples, and make them humorous. "This lesson is easier than catching fish in a barrel with a large butterfly net."

☺ When assigning homework, have you ever told students that "practice makes perfect"? Does anyone actually know someone who is perfect? No. Practice actually makes improvement. Look for amusing anecdotes that can be used to illustrate difficult concepts. Listed below are a few examples you can use.

***Strive for Perfection—or Else!***  Data tell us that we all make mistakes and are not perfect, but that we need to strive for perfection. If 99.9 percent is good enough, then

1. 2 million documents will be lost by the IRS this year;
2. 22,000 checks will be deducted from the wrong bank accounts in the next 60 minutes;
3. 12 babies will be given to the wrong parents each day;
4. 2,488,200 books will be shipped in the next 12 months with the wrong cover;
5. 291 pacemaker operations will be performed incorrectly this year;
6. 880,000 credit cards in circulation will turn out to have incorrect cardholder information on their magnetic strips;
7. 55 malfunctioning automatic teller machines will be installed in the next 12 months;
8. 20,000 incorrect drug prescriptions will be written in the next 12 months;
9. 107 incorrect medical procedures will be performed by the end of the day today;
10. 315 entries in Webster's Third New International Dictionary of the English Language will turn out to be misspelled. (InSight, Syncurde Canada Ltd., Communications Division, 1998).

## Action Step 2: Develop a Joking Relationship with Students to Help with Engagement, Learning, and Behavior

It is not such a tall order to learn humor; use it to develop relationships, increase engagement, and improve behavior. If you force it, it does not happen. However, apt and relevant humor does in fact develop true relationships with students. These relationships in turn serve as a mechanism of social control and a tension-reducing device (Bricker, 1980). Coleman (1992) suggests the following:

1. The more humor, the better for children.
2. Nonrelated humor can be very effective with children, even more so than more sophisticated related humor such as irony and satire. However, the older the student, the more related the humor should be to the material.
3. As the child matures in terms of intellectual development, nonrelated humor becomes less effective in terms of information acquisition and retention.
4. Use of some nonrelated humor, such as irony and satire, can have a negative effect on a child's information acquisition.
5. For adults, use of nonrelated humor can have at least no effect and at worse a negative effect.
6. Use of nonrelated humor for adults can negatively affect student-teacher rapport, while the use of relevant humor makes learning more enjoyable (p. 274).

## Action Step 3: Be Careful Not to Joke All the Time; This Can Turn Students into Class Clowns and You May Lose Control

The use of humor is great, but as noted previously, there does have to be a limit. No one knows for sure how much is too much, but it appears that three to five jokes, or events, per hour seem to be about right for older students. A teacher who allows a lot of unrestrained laughter in class runs the risk of losing control. Once again, the key may be to watch your students: their actions and verbal and nonverbal cues will let you know to increase or decrease the amount of humor being used.

Bivens et al. (1998) note that teachers must be "models of playful-ness." Try new behaviors, do not be afraid to laugh at your own mis-takes, be open to children's "fanciful" ideas, and convey the sense that learning can be fun. If you are afraid of failing, I suggest you eat a live toad in the morning and nothing worse will happen to you for the rest of the day. As the teacher, you set the tone in class. If it is time to be serious, you need to model this behavior. Of course, it may be true that the teacher who is smiling when things go wrong . . . has already thought of someone else to blame.

## Practical Examples

"Humor reinforces the absurdity of rigid, inflexible behavior and misunderstanding and helps us remember that mistakes are natural and widespread in all humanity" (Weinstein, 1986; Berger, 1999; Crawford, 1994b; Wallinger, 1997, p. 31). The days of dictatorial teachers are gone. Humor breaks down the old industrial barriers of top-down teaching.

1. A picture is worth a thousand words, but a good story is worth a thousand lectures.
2. Post cartoons throughout the classroom, the more related to the subject, the better.
3. Let students make a mascot for class.
4. Collect and use well-known proverbs—a proverb saved is a prov-erb learned.
5. Humor should differ according to the age and personality of the student. Be playful, use exaggeration, and tell stories and amusing anecdotes (Stephenson and Thibault, 2006, p. 65).

## Action Step 4: Lessons Learned from Bowling

Robert Putnam's book *Bowling Alone* draws on vast amounts of data from national surveys that report on Americans' changing behaviors over the past twenty-five years. Putnam recognizes that years ago, Americans bowled in organized leagues, usually after work; they no longer do this. This seemingly small phenomenon symbolizes a sig-nificant social change. Putnam concludes that Americans have become disconnected from family, friends, neighbors, and social structures, as he points to the shrinking access to the "social capital" that is the reward of communal activity. The decrease in community sharing is a serious threat to our civic and personal health. While humor may not be able to fix the social ills of society, it is a start in building "humor capital" to replace the "social capital." For example, Putnam's book points out how we have become increasingly disconnected from one another and how social structures have disintegrated. The social fabric of America has changed over the last few decades as a loss of social bonds has affected the attitude, education, health, and safety of individuals. If this trend does not push us to use more humor, nothing will.

Humor can be used as a motivational tool in the classroom, but it also helps build teamwork and social capital. Good-natured joking about a mistake puts individuals at ease, and leaders who use humor when they make a mistake help to motivate others to try something new and take chances. Remember, an ounce of pretension is worth a pound of manure.

## Practical Examples

☺ Will Rogers wrote that "there's no trick to being a humorist when you have the whole government working for you." Use political satire in class.

☺ Use overhead transparencies to make a point. Have pictures, charts, cartoons, and expressions ready to use.

 1. A jumper cable walks into a bar. The bartender says, "I'll serve you, but don't start anything."
 2. Two peanuts walk into a bar, and one was a salted.
 3. A man walks into a bar with a slab of asphalt under his arm and says, "A beer please, and one for the road."
 4. Two cannibals are eating a clown. One says to the other, "Does this taste funny to you?"

## Action Step 5: Lessons from the Brain

Eric Jensen writes in *Phi Delta Kappan* that social conditions actually influence the brain. A new emerging discipline called *social neuroscience* entails the exploration of how social conditions affect the brain. Jensen writes that "school behaviors are highly social experiences, which become encoded through our sense of reward, acceptance, pain, pleasure, coherence, affinity, and stress. This understanding suggests that we be more active in managing the social environment of students" (Jensen, 2008, p. 411). Consequently, humor helps build social networks, social networks influence the brain, and then the brain is affected by emotional intelligence—hence the connection of humor, the brain, and student behavior: it all comes full circle to improve learning from many different angles. The brain is able to rewire and remap itself by means of neuroplasticity. This means that the right balance of humor, emotion, and learning can make positive and significant changes in our brains in a short time.

### Action Step 6: Use Humor to Uphold Standards, but Also Be Flexible

One of the most important rules for teachers is to develop genuine relationships with students while being themselves. Students want rules to follow and it is up to teachers to uphold standards, but this must be done naturally, and possibly with a little bit of humor (ASCD, 2001, p. 5). Humor can certainly be used to enforce rules, make fun of rigid guidelines, and even help us remember that mistakes are natural and widespread in all humanity (Weinstein, 1986; Berger, 1999; Crawford, 1994b; Wallinger, 1997).

As with any good lesson plan, the key here is to be prepared. Develop a list of jokes, stories, anecdotes, and so forth, that you can readily access for addressing the behavior of students in a multiplicity of situations. Writing down jokes or interesting stories in lesson plans will take some behavioral adjustments; however, it is not easy to talk yourself into actions that you have behaved yourself out of.

☺ Use this "e-mail from God" to tell students when they are misbehaving.

One day God was looking down at Earth and saw all the evil that was going on. He decided to send an angel down to Earth to check it out. So, he called on a female angel and sent her to Earth for a time. When she returned she told God, "Yes, it is bad on Earth; 95 percent of the people are bad and 5 percent are good."

God said, "This is not good." He decided to e-mail the 5 percent who were good and encourage them, just a little something to help them keep going. Do you know what the e-mail said? Oh, you didn't get one either?

Ultimately, teachers who are able to use brief and pointed humor as a teaching strategy aimed at students are able to decrease anger in the classroom and affect the overall behavior in class (Forbes, 1997; Edwards and Gibboney, 1992; Gorham and Christophel, 1990).

Listed below is another story you may want to use. Students will stop talking and listen to a story if for no other reason than to hear the ending.

***Abbott and Costello's Computer Conversation*** If Bud Abbott and Lou Costello were alive today, their famous sketch, "Who's on first?" might have turned out something like this:

COSTELLO calls to buy a computer from ABBOTT.

ABBOTT: Super Duper computer store. Can I help you?

COSTELLO: Thanks. I'm setting up an office in my den and I'm thinking about buying a computer.

ABBOTT: Mac?

COSTELLO: No, the name's Lou.

ABBOTT: Your computer?

COSTELLO: I don't own a computer. I want to buy one.

ABBOTT: Mac?

COSTELLO: I told you, my name's Lou.

ABBOTT: What about Windows?

COSTELLO: Why? Will it get stuffy in here?

ABBOTT: Do you want a computer with Windows?

COSTELLO: I don't know. What will I see when I look at the windows?

ABBOTT: Wallpaper.

COSTELLO: Never mind the windows. I need a computer and software.

ABBOTT: Software for Windows?

COSTELLO: No. On the computer! I need something I can use to write proposals, track expenses, and run my business. What do you have?

ABBOTT: Office.

COSTELLO: Yeah, for my office. Can you recommend anything?

ABBOTT: I just did.

## Practical Examples

☺  If I have a good enough relationship with students, I will spray them with water from a bottle when they are misbehaving.

☺  Put Jack Handey "deep thoughts" quotes on the board every day. Here is the website: www.deepthoughtsbyjackhandey.com/.

☺  Throughout the day, there are going to be times when you are confused, your students are confused, or your staff is confused. Do not hide it; joke about it. Harry S. Truman said, "If you cannot convince them, confuse them." Too many times teachers try to cover up the unknown by pretending to know the answer or by just ignoring the problem. The best way to solve a problem, resolve a conflict, or ease the confusion is to hit the situation head-on. Have standard lines to use when you are confused, for example, "OK, I meant to confuse you here, did it work?" or "How many people are as confused as I am at this point?"

☺  Use interesting historical lessons to make your point. For example, the term "trivia" comes from the Middle Ages and refers to the place where three roads (tri or trivium) would come together. It was at this point that the most amount of traffic would pass. Therefore, people usually posted notes and messages at this location. Hence the word *trivia*.

# 9

# HUMOR HELPS TEACHERS MAINTAIN INTEREST AT WORK

How is it that we put a man on the moon before we figured out it would be a good idea to put wheels on luggage?

—Anonymous

**W**hen in class, you must be enthusiastic because students can tell if you are not being sincere. Remember, you must love what you do, but do not show fear. Students or colleagues can be like sharks and attack the fearful. It's just like the line in the movie *The Santa Clause* 2: "Seeing isn't believing, believing is seeing." (This movie is a classic if there ever was one, but go ahead and admit it, you did not even know there was a *Santa Clause* 1 movie.) I used to say that when hiring new faculty I had to ask only one question: "Why do you want to work such long hours, for very little compensation and few rewards, and have critics watching your every move?" If the candidates could convince me that the benefits far outweighed the negatives, they could be hired. But if they could do it with enthusiasm, they had to be hired. However, keeping that initial enthusiasm of new teachers is tricky. One way to help is to develop morale, motivation, and job satisfaction through a positive work environment built on humor. Keith Harrell, a motivational speaker, used to work for a large computer company.

He tells the story of how one day the head of the human resources department brought everyone together to announce large layoffs (almost 80 percent of the workforce) because of a poor economy. Keith immediately raised his hand and said, "I have a question. After these 80 percent are gone, can I have a bigger office?" The right attitude is key to making work fun.

## RESEARCH AND THEORY

In 2001, B. Lee Hurren completed a dissertation, "The Effects of Principals' Humor on Teachers' Job Satisfaction," which measured principals' use of humor and job satisfaction for 471 elementary, middle, and secondary school teachers in Nevada. Hurren studied various situations and found significant differences in teacher job satisfaction based on the frequency of humor used by principals. Humor increases job satisfaction in schools, no matter what the grade level or size of the school.

In support of these findings, Koonce (1997) administered two different instruments to 951 elementary school teachers employed at 25 elementary schools in the Chesapeake Public Schools Division in the Commonwealth of Virginia. Receiving a 60 percent response rate, Koonce utilized descriptive and inferential statistics to find that school climate is affected by the principals' humor style, with an approximate effect size of 1.04 (large). Koonce also found that male principals are more often the producer and reproducer of humor style than female principals, at a rate of almost 2 to 1 (statistically significant at 0.05 level). Moreover, the tenure of the principal is related to teacher perception of the principal's humor style. The younger principals used humor more. Hopefully, the statistics in this study make sense, because "the manipulation of statistical formulas is no substitute for knowing what one is doing." ~ Hubert M. Blalock Jr.

Putting these empirical studies together, it becomes apparent that when humor is encouraged in schools, it provides for a better working environment where teachers are more satisfied, students are more engaged, and subsequently there is a higher-quality learning environment.

## Action Step 1: Principals Who Use Humor Increase Their Leadership

Marken (1999) and others have argued that humor is a behavior that contributes to the enhancement of school leadership.

1. Principals are more likely to gain the support and participation of their teachers and staff when they use humor.
2. Humor has a positive, humanizing effect on the principal; this can decrease authority barriers.
3. Humor helps principals maintain a more balanced perspective.
4. Principals will maintain a more positive tone at the school when they use humor.
5. Humor contributes to the effectiveness of the principal's leadership at the school site.

Hurren (2001) concluded that the more principals use humor, the more teachers are satisfied in their jobs. Of course, this conclusion is based on the available statistics, and we all know that 42.7 percent of all statistics are made up on the spot—just kidding.

## Practical Examples

☺ Allow individuals to decorate their offices any way they want. This allows individuals freedom of expression. I work with an advertising agency that has a Ping-Pong table, complete with bleachers, in the middle of the meeting room. One staff member has his desk made up to look like the front of a car, with a stuffed deer on the floor in front to make it look like the "car" has hit the deer. Another man has his office designed as a museum with a tag on every item indicating who donated it, along with a "for sale" tag; the tags are on the lamp, desk, chair, and so forth. This liberty is great for morale and staff empowerment.

☺ Start school meetings with a lie. Have everyone take turns telling a lie to start a class, a meeting, or general group activity. In fact, Burlington, Wisconsin, has a liars' club that organizes an annual contest to crown the World's Greatest Liar. Here are a few of the better recent entries:

1. "The Wisconsin River was so low this year that the local government started taxing us for more property on our riverfront lot." Greg M. Peck, Janesville, Wisconsin.
2. Longtime member Tom Balza of Appleton wrote: "My cooking is a problem with my new stove. I cannot double my recipes: my oven will not go up to 700 degrees F."
3. David Laing of Milwaukee tells us, "I'm so lonely I drive down one-way streets the wrong way, just to get someone to wave to me."
4. Mardy Nersesian of Racine has some golf issues: "I had so many divots this past summer, the government named three golf courses federal disaster areas." (www.burling-tonliarsclub.com/, retrieved 3/5/08)

☺ Bring in a comedian or improvisational troupe as part of professional development. This type of "training" will not only add to the culture of the organization, but it sends a strong message that humor is perfectly acceptable.

## Action Step 2: Teachers Who Use Humor Gain Control of Themselves and Their Classroom

If teachers are encouraged and guided to use humor, they can gain a sense of control in their life. The use of humor represents what some researchers call *cognitive control* (Wooten, 1996). True cognitive control of humor is similar to a well-prepared teacher who breeds confidence when he knows the material and has a true handle on teaching techniques. Obviously, this type of confidence comes with time and practice.

## Practical Examples

☺ Develop humor policies for your class or school. The rules can be used to set guidelines for groups to help prevent outrageous behavior, but they also help to establish a culture of humor. For example, if you are late for a meeting, you need to tell one knock knock joke.

☺   Have a professional-development day on integrating humor into the classroom by reading the same funny book. Have everyone purchase this book—I need the royalties!

☺   Not every teacher or student will know how to integrate humor into the classroom. Here are some easy-to-follow steps that may help.

1. Change takes time; after all, Lambeau Field was not built in a day—can you guess I am a Green Bay Packers fan?
2. Start changing the environment yourself, and then look for volunteers to help integrating humor.
3. I suggest that teachers meet monthly for at least seventy-five minutes to discuss how to integrate humor.
4. Teachers should meet in groups of eight to ten to discuss new ideas for using humor.
5. Have teachers meet in similar groups, for example, similar subjects.
6. Establish building-based groups to discuss ideas that work.
7. Have teachers make detailed, modest, individual action plans to use humor.
8. Bring in a facilitator to help with the process of integrating humor into the classroom.

## Action Step 3: What Makes "Good" Teachers?

This one particular question has been the topic of many books. There may be as many answers as questions regarding the behaviors, characteristics, or skills needed to be a successful teacher, but one fact remains constant: if you have quality teachers in the classroom, everything else seems to work better, for example, technology, standardized tests, behavior, and so forth. Connected to this fact is that humor constantly ranks as an important characteristic of successful teachers (see Krisko, 2001).

## Practical Examples

***Rules to Live By . . .***    Every organization, group of kids, and school has its own clichés used on a daily basis. Learn to speak the language of the group so as to include it in the humor.

In humor, there is a rule of "threes." Whenever you use a list, include three items. The first two items should be normal, with the last one being the unexpected, or funny, item. For example, there are three things you need to know about homework: (1) it helps students learn the material, (2) practice makes perfect, and (3) parents appreciate homework so they can finally get the TV. By the way, why are you *in* a movie, but you're *on* TV?

Another rule of thumb is to set up the joke, get in, and get out. In other words, relate the joke or humorous activity to the content of your message and then move on. Remember, people are intelligent—they can understand your point and do not need something dwelled on for hours.

The final rule to remember is that humor must be connected to the content in order to be useful. In fact, the following simple model explains that humor must be used at the appropriate opportunity, related to the content of the material, and placed in the correct context in regard to the environment and audience. Remember that the squeeze is more important than the juice.

☺   Use a "time machine" in class. You do not have to build a real time machine for this to work, although that would be more interesting. Students love stepping into a time machine to "get into" character. This can be used in a multiplicity of settings, ranging from history courses to English and even math when students make presentations or simply need to learn more about topics (e.g., leadership). "What we know today does not make what we did yesterday wrong; it makes tomorrow better."

☺   Put a cartoon on the bathroom pass.

☺   Collect poor or unusual answers of students on tests from years gone by and use them as examples in class for a test review. Be sure to use the examples after the student has graduated, or have a good lawyer handy.

☺   When you make a mistake, own up to it and just call it a Freudian slip.

☺   Develop humorous web pages for your classes.

☺   Knock knock jokes and lightbulb jokes are good in almost any situation partially because the context can be changed to fit the situation. For example, how many ballerinas does it take to change a lightbulb? One, but she has to stand on a chair and hold onto the lightbulb while she waits for the world to revolve around her. Wherever you are, you can take out the word *ballerina* and replace it with a term related to your class or speech. When talking with teachers you can use the following: How many school administrators does it take to change a lightbulb? One this year, two next year, and we budgeted for four the following year. How many teachers does it take to change a lightbulb? Change??

All these activities may be challenging but they help teachers keep their enthusiasm for the job. Research tells us that too many teachers leave the profession from burnout. Integrating new challenges like humor should help counteract this fact. It is a little like the information that I present to students when I am about to lecture them:

Research indicates that

- ☺ after 10 minutes, 10 percent of you will be drifting off;
- ☺ after 15 minutes, 10 percent more of the class will be taking mental vacations;
- ☺ after 20 minutes, another 25 percent will be dreaming of sexual fantasies;
- ☺ so, I have no apologies for the pleasure I am about to give 25 percent of you.

## Action Step 4: Developing the Characteristic of Humor Leads to Teacher Satisfaction, Motivation, and More Productivity

Haugen and Melhus (2006) write that there are three stages of satisfaction in an organization. The first level is where satisfaction is the foundation of the employees' relationship with an organization. There must be a certain order in their existence at work before they can move on to the next stage. Goals and visions in an organization are the essence of existence and should provide answers to why we are here, who we are here for, and which direction we should go. Enthusiasm is the third stage of satisfaction leading to a long-term success for the organization. Employees must be motivated individually and collectively in order to make the move toward improved results. Satisfaction, enthusiasm, and motivation can all be improved through humor, thereby increasing retention of teachers and moving the school forward in the achievement of goals. Or you could follow the advice of Drew Carey: "Oh, you hate your job? Why didn't you say so? There's a support group for that. It's called *everybody*, and they meet at the bar."

Agreeing with the work of Haugen and Melhus are Davis and Kleiner (1989), who led a group of researchers who believe humor has a multiplicity of practical benefits including the following: it reduces stress, helps employees understand management's concerns, and motivates employees. Principals who use humor not only contribute to the enjoyment of teachers but also help teachers and students pursue their goals. Ultimately, higher motivation and job satisfaction result in greater teacher productivity (Ziegler, Boardman, and Thomas, 1985; Hurren, 2001). "Believe those who seek the truth, doubt those who find it." ~ Zen saying.

## Action Step 5: When Used on a Consistent Basis, Humor Not Only Reduces Tension, but Provides a Coping Mechanism and Eventually Helps with Teacher Burnout

It must be noted that teachers use "humor to help themselves, usually to help them maintain their interest or to reduce their own tension" (Rareshide, 1993, p. 18). Teachers must exercise their "humor in a positive way to have a personal magnetism that draws others to them. People like to feel good, be complimented for their success, and exist in a world free from tension and strain. Humor has the ability to assist all these goals" (Wallinger, 1997, p. 34).

Teachers can use humor as a coping mechanism to help handle the stress of their job. It serves as a relief for emotional exhaustion, and while the end result is somewhat circuitous, humor is one variable that helps prevent occupational burnout (Tumkaya, 2007). Humor could even help bring about world peace if used appropriately (this one may be a bit of an exaggeration).

### Practical Examples

1. Learn humor through immersion (like taking a bath). Read everything you can about humor and teaching.

2. Learn different types of humor: researchers have identified almost one hundred different types or techniques of humor, from the wisecrack to riddles to Freudian slips. For example, you can actually buy Freudian slip sticky notes to use in class. They are great conversation pieces.

3. Learn about comedy writers or storytellers. Michael Hodgin's *1001 More Humorous Illustrations for Public Speaking: Fresh, Timely, and Compelling Illustrations for Preachers, Teachers, and Speakers* is a good resource.

4. Read books on public speakers and take notes on successful and funny speakers.

5. Expose yourself to humor on a regular basis and create a humor library.

6. Go on the Internet and steal information. Remember, good research is nothing more than legalized plagiarism.

7. Have students create humorous definitions of words.

8. Do humor exercises. Metcalf and Felible (1992) recommend doing "humoraerobics," which are silly noises, peculiar gestures, and funny faces that allow you to take risks with your appearance.

9. Take humor breaks in class.

10. Decorate your office with humorous items (Brooks, 1992). For example, my office at Stritch has a six-foot-tall blow-up figure of the Incredible Hulk. He is there to keep students in line.

## VIDEAGOGY

*Pedagogy* may be defined as the art, science, or profession of teaching. Obviously, there are numerous teaching styles and methods that have proven successful over the years. Let me introduce to you the use of short videos in class, or *pedagogy plus videos = videagogy*. A key aspect of utilizing humor is to use visual effects with teaching. Teaching with the use of short videos is not only a fun way to integrate humor but also is a great way to integrate technology; it thus matches the learning style of many young students, and even connects with Gardner's theory of multiple intelligences.

TV commercials are the best, but YouTube, collegehumor.com/video, MySpace, and video.google.com are sites filled with numerous videos that work well in class. One of the best things is that these videos tend to run from thirty seconds to only a few minutes, which is long enough to get the point home but short enough not to bore the audience. Short videos of a few seconds to less than five minutes work best. Build a video library on a notebook computer that can be utilized at any time. Use the humorous videos for a humor break or to emphasize your point about the course content. Categorize the videos by main topic so you can find one for the main lessons. Let me give you a few examples that work well.

There is a commercial for the European lotto that has a taxi driver stopping in front of a crowd of people. Everyone wants a ride, but the driver is discerning. He turns on the radio and starts lip-synching the song, "Ballroom Blitz" by Sweet. Everyone on the curb seems confused except one individual who "gets it." The man starts lip-synching the song along with the taxi driver, who ultimately offers the gentleman a ride. Off they go—much to the dismay of everyone else waiting. The commercial fades out and says, "Lotto millionaires are not like ordinary millionaires." Every time I show the video, people love it, and it can then be used for discussions on topics such as why we do not have to follow the norm, or how there are topics that some people "get" and others simply do not understand. The bottom line with videagogy is that you find short videos that make people look, listen, think, and discuss—it is called critical thinking and is a great use of technology.

Another example is a video of the U.S. women's soccer team in a dentist's office. Mia Hamm comes out with the dentist, who explains that Mia has two cavities. One by one, each member of the soccer team stands and proclaims, "Then I will have two fillings," even though the dentist explains that he just examined them all and they were fine. In the end, the receptionist stands and says, "And then I will have two fillings." The words "We will take on the world, as a team" come onto the screen, along with the Nike emblem. This is a wonderful sixty-second video depicting teamwork. The video can be followed by a discussion of cooperation and teamwork.

There are thousands and thousands of videos on YouTube that work well for teaching. You simply have to take the time to look them over and be a little creative about how to use them in class. Interspersing several of these short videos into a lesson plan or speech is an excellent and funny way to liven up the classroom while utilizing brain-research techniques. And the research indicates that students will remember the information better and longer with the use of videos and humor.

## COPYRIGHT CONSIDERATIONS

With the advent of more technology, advanced search tools, and an increased number of Internet sites such as YouTube, Yahoo, Google, and so forth, it is important to remember that authors follow copyright rules. New guidelines for information sharing, downloading, Twittering, and so forth, are emerging every day. However, it is important that educators not fall under the tyranny of supposed "experts" who randomly present at conferences, providing unduly strict copyright guidelines and scaring many of those in attendance. One credible source is the Code of Best Practices in Fair Use for Media Literacy Education, produced by Temple University and found at centerforsocialmedia.org/medialiteracy. This research paper properly defines the Fair Use code in education.

> Fair use is the part of copyright law that permits new makers, in some situations, to quote copyrighted material without asking permission or paying the owners. The courts tell us that fair use should be "transformative"—adding value to what they take and using it for a purpose different from the original work. (www.centerforsocialmedia.org/resources/publications/recut_reframe_recycle/)

## (10)

# CONCLUSION

Conclusions are supposed to summarize information from the previous chapters, and if this were completely accurate you would really only need to read the final chapter of any book—maybe this is true after all. So, here are a few lists to live by.

## QUICK FACTS TO KNOW ABOUT USING HUMOR

1. Always relate the jokes to the audience and material.
2. Do not let your message get lost in the joke.
3. Get in and get out. Tell the joke, relate it to your text, and move on.
4. Tailor the jokes and activities to the size of the group, level of expertise, and culture. This means you need to do some homework and find these things out.
5. Many individuals use humor as the sword that cuts. Using sarcasm to cut down others, to make fun of people, or to ridicule may get a laugh, but it is almost always destructive when building relationships. The only time that cutting humor may work is when you have a very close relationship with the target of your joke and the

audience knows about the close relationship; otherwise, stay away from criticizing others with humor.

## GUIDELINES FOR USING HUMOR IN A MULTICULTURAL WORLD

Simons (1997) lists several guidelines for using humor in a multicultural world, thereby enhancing the climate of any organization.

1. First-person experiences are usually the best because they help relate a human side of the story and will be less offensive to others.
2. People should use humor to lighten a delicate or controversial situation, not make fun of it. No one likes to be the target of someone else's humor—sorry, Don Rickles. People can bond by sharing humor.
3. Ask others for their perspective on a situation or any humorous story, and they immediately become part of the group. For example, when you have a new class, ask them to say a little something about their strengths and goals or aspirations and then ask them for an interesting, unique, or humorous story about themselves. As the teacher you should go first; the activity then makes the students more comfortable and, hopefully, more emotionally stable in a sometimes-stressful environment. Study humor.
4. There are numerous Internet sites that provide jokes of the day or interesting stories that can be used to help with the culture of the class. Just like teaching, using humor takes preparation, and just like teaching, the same lesson plans do not work year after year, nor do the same tired jokes. Why did the chicken cross the road? Because he was too lazy to find a new ending to the story. You get my point (Simons, 1997, p. 2).

## CAUTIONS FOR USING HUMOR

Like using hazardous material, using humor should come with a few warnings and cautions that need to be addressed before you try to be funny without a net:

1. Humor should not be avoided; simply approach humor with respect for the person.
2. Minimize the offensive nature of joking by avoiding jokes that discriminate against people (but not lawyers).
3. Aggressive, put-down humor should be avoided.
4. A climate of reciprocal humor should be encouraged.
5. Keep the humor relevant to the situation/context.
6. Make sure that the humor reflects the interests and language of the followers.
7. Make the humor brief and conversational.
8. If delivered in address form, humor must be adapted to a conversational tone, not a written tone.
9. Use self-effacing humor if the situation warrants (this will give you high credibility).
10. Take your message seriously, but don't take yourself too seriously.
11. Remember to attack the position, not the person's dignity, through humor.
12. Avoid inconsistent humor; it's better that people think that you have no sense of humor than to attack them or not have them understand your line of reasoning.
13. Avoid topics that center around sex, illegal activities, or other organizational topics that are taboo (Alinea group, www.alinea-group.com/Leaders%20Humor.htm).
14. Self-disparaging humor will enhance the leader's image, while self-promoting humor has the opposite effect (adapted from Gruner, 1985, p. 142).
15. When using humorous satire in a form of communication, be sure to know the level of intelligence of your audience (adapted from Gruner, 1985, p. 144).

And now, if you remember nothing else, here are Jonas's Ten Laws of Humor—the Final Word (thank goodness):

1. Develop a database of jokes, stories, sayings, and so on. Every time you go to a conference, hear a speech, or even watch TV, take notes and be sure to add the stories to your database. Be religious about this activity. Be sure to categorize information for easy use.

With modern technology there are 101 ways to do this, from using a PDA to even using cell phones. You can even leave yourself phone messages about a joke or story that you hear so you can put it into the file later on.

2. You do not have to reinvent the wheel. Search the Internet and read great books (like this one) to get fresh material. Or just borrow the information. One of the goals of this book is to provide you with jokes, stories, and other material embedded in the text.

3. Always look for connections with your material. Do not just cut out a cute cartoon or funny joke. Write a short note on the back where it may fit in with your material or activities. You will be grateful later.

4. As you complete a lesson plan or plan an organizational meeting, be sure to plot out the jokes, stories, humorous transparencies, and so forth. Look spontaneous and be prepared. Humor can be learned and planned; it does not have to be extemporaneous. I actually outline my lectures and write in the jokes in the places where they should work the best.

5. Collect overhead transparencies and be sure to label them or categorize them. Share jokes and cartoons with your colleagues; they will return the favor. The overhead is a great way to make a point, get someone's attention, and leave a visual impact on a class. Keep a three-ring binder of transparencies or scan them onto a flash drive. (Sometimes I wear a necklace with a CD on the end of it around my neck. I do this and explain that this is how silly it looks when people wear a flash drive around their necks—it is *not* jewelry.) I carry the transparencies to class almost every day, just in case. In fact, there are three questions that you can get from students: "good" questions, "great" questions, and "excellent" questions. "Good" questions are the ones that you do not know the answer to, so you make up something to stall while you think of a good response, like explaining there are three different kinds of questions. "Great" questions are the ones that you know the answer to. And "excellent" questions are the ones that you know the answer to, and have a transparency to demonstrate. Be prepared.

6. Keep track of the reactions you get with various jokes, stories, and activities. This will take some work, but any improvement takes time. Of course, go ahead and reuse the jokes that work and do

not be afraid to eliminate the ones that don't, even if you think they are funny.

7. Look at reality for some of the funniest things to discuss and use. Students love to learn more about practical aspects of the theoretical knowledge, and they certainly will be able to make more connections between humor and knowledge from real-life situations (more brain stuff). Here is a "true" story, (supposedly) from the Internet.

> The following is an actual question given on a University of Washington chemistry midterm. The answer by one student was so "profound" that the professor shared it with colleagues, via the Internet, which is, of course, why we now have the pleasure of enjoying it as well.
>
> Bonus question: Is hell exothermic (gives off heat) or endothermic (absorbs heat)? Most of the students wrote proofs of their beliefs using Boyle's law (gas cools off when it expands and heats up when it is compressed) or some variant. One student, however, wrote the following:
>
> "First, we need to know how the mass of hell is changing in time. So, we need to know the rate that souls are moving into hell and the rate they are leaving. I think that we can safely assume that once a soul gets to hell, it will not leave. Therefore, no souls are leaving. As for how many souls are entering hell, let's look at the different religions that exist in the world today. Most of these religions state that if you are not a member of their religion, you will go to hell. Since there is more than one of these religions and since people do not belong to more than one religion, we can project that all souls go to hell. With birth and death rates as they are, we can expect the number of souls in hell to increase exponentially. Now, we look at the rate of change of the volume in hell because Boyle's law states that in order for the temperature and pressure in hell to stay the same, the volume of hell has to expand proportionately as souls are added. This gives two possibilities: (1) If hell is expanding at a slower rate than the rate at which souls enter hell, then the temperature and pressure in hell will increase until all hell breaks loose, and (2) if hell is expanding at a rate faster than the increase of souls in hell, then the temperature and pressure will drop until hell freezes over. So which is it? If we accept the postulate given to me by Theresa during my freshman year, "that it will be a cold day in hell before I go out with you," and take into account the fact that I still have not succeeded in having a date with her, then #2 above cannot be true, and thus I am sure that hell is exothermic and will not freeze over." Supposedly, this student received an A.

8. Do not be afraid to encourage students to develop a sense of humor in class. Humor can be very contagious—let it happen. This will mean "letting go" of some power of being a teacher, but it will be worth the effort. Let students tell jokes in class. Let your staff tell jokes.

9. Just do it. Don't be afraid to make mistakes and look less than perfect. Staff and students will respect you for the chances you take, if not for your knowledge and sense of humor.

10. Be sure that you have tenure (or a strong union) before you try any of the suggestions in this book, or at least a second career to fall back on.

# REFERENCES

Ackroyd, S., and P. Thompson. (1999). *Organisational misbehavior*. Thousand Oaks, CA: Sage.

Adams, S. (1996). *The Dilbert Principle: A cubicle's-eye view of bosses, meetings, management fads, and other workplace afflictions*. New York: United Media.

Allport, G. W. (1961). *Pattern and growth in personality*. New York: Harcourt College Publishers.

Arch, D. (1996). *Red hot handouts! Taking the Ho Hum out of handouts*. San Francisco: Jossey-Bass.

Aria, C. (2002). The use of humor in vocabulary instruction. Master's thesis, Kean Univ.

ASCD. (2001). Make me laugh: Using humor in the classroom. *ASCD education update*. Retrieved 3/14/07 from www.teacheq.com/images/IEILArticle-HumorSchool.pdf.

Association for Applied and Therapeutic Humor. (n.d.). Retrieved 10/8/06 from www.aath.org.

Aylor, B., and P. Oppliger. (2003). Out-of-class communication and student perceptions of instructor humor orientation and socio-communicative style. *Communication Education* 52 (2): 122–34.

Avolio, B., J. M. Howell, and J. J. Sosik. (1999). A funny thing happened on the way to the bottom line: Humour as a moderator of leadership style effects. *Academy of Management Journal* 42 (2): 219–27.

Azim, E., D. Mobbs, B. Jo, V. Menon, and A. Reiss. (2005). Sex differences in brain activation elicited by humor. *Proceedings of the National Academy of Sciences*. Retrieved 12/7/08 from www.pnas.org/content/102/45/16496.full.

Bacall, A. (2002). *The lighter side of educational leadership*. Thousand Oaks, CA: Corwin Press.

Banning, M. R., and D. L. Nelson. (1987). The effects of activity-elicited humor and group structure on group cohesion and affective structure on group cohesion and affective responses. *American Journal of Occupational Therapy* 41 (8): 510–14.

Barlow, C., J. Blythe, and M. Edmonds. (1998). *A handbook of interactive exercises for groups*. Needham Heights, MA: Allyn & Bacon.

Begley, S. (2000). The science of laughs: Scanning brains and eavesdropping on chimps, researchers are figuring out why we chuckle, guffaw and crack up. Hint: it isn't funny. *Newsweek*, October 9. Retrieved 12/7/08 from www. accessmylibrary.com/coms2/summary_0286-28396406_ITM.

Bennis, W. G. (1959). Leadership theory and administrative behavior: The problem of authority. *Administrative Science Quarterly* 4:259–301.

———. (1989). *On becoming a leader*. Reading, MA: Addison-Wesley.

———. (1996). The Leader as storyteller. *Harvard Business Review*, reprint 96102, 1–6.

Berger, A. A. (1999). *An anatomy of humor*. New Brunswick, NJ: Transaction Publishers.

Berk, R. A. (1996). Student rating of 10 strategies for using humor in college teaching. *Journal on Excellence in College Teaching* 7 (3): 71–92.

———. (2000). Does humor in course tests reduce anxiety and improve performance? *College Teaching* 48 (4): 151–58.

———. (2002). *Humor as an instructional defibrillator: Evidence-based techniques in teaching and assessment*. Sterling, VA: Stylus.

———. (2003). *Professors are from Mars, students are from Snickers: How to write and deliver humor in the classroom and in professional presentations*. Sterling, VA: Stylus.

Berk, R. A., and J. Nanda. (2006). A randomized trial of humor effects on test anxiety and test performance. *Humor* 19 (4): 425–54.

Berkowitz, L. (1970). Aggressive humor as a stimulus to aggressive responses. *Journal of Personality and Social Psychology* 16 (4): 710–17.

Binderman, M. (2002). Humor as a healing tool. Retrieved 1/7/04 from www. aotf.org/html/humor.html

Bippus, A. (2007). Factors predicting the perceived effectiveness of politicians' use of humor during a debate. *HUMOR: International Journal of Humor Research* 20 (2): 105–21.

Bivens, A., et al. (1998). Humor and learning: A group project. Retrieved 1/7/04 from www.users.muohio.edu/shermalw/ EDP603SM2005/EDP603_ GROUPHUMOR.HTMLX.

Blau, P. M. (1963). *The dynamics of bureaucracy: A study of interpersonal relations in two government agencies*. Rev. ed. Chicago: University of Chicago Press.

Boland, R. J., and R. Hoffman. (1982). Humor in a machine shop: An interpretation of symbolic action. In *Organizational reality: Reports from the firing line*, ed. P. J. Frost, V. F. Mitchell, and W. R. Nord, 372–77. Glenview, IL: Scott Foresman.

Bolinger, B. S. (2001). Humor and leadership: A gender-based investigation of the correlation between the attribute of humor and effective leadership. PhD diss., Indiana State Univ.

Bradney, P. (1957). The joking relationship in industry. *Human Relations* 10 (2): 179–87.

Bricker, V. R. (1980). The function of humor in Zinacantan. *Journal of Anthropological Research* 36 (4): 411–18.

Brooks, G. P. (1991). Functions of humor in small group communication: The relationship of the use of humor to group task, group effectiveness, group cohesiveness, and group communication satisfaction. Master's thesis, Ohio Univ.

———. (1992). Humor in leadership: State of the art in theory and practice. Paper presented at the annual meeting of the Mid-Western Education Research Association, Chicago.

Brown, G. E., P. A. Dixon, and J. D. Hudson. (1982). Effect of peer pressure on imitation of humor response in college students. *Psychological Reports* 51:1111–17.

Bryant, J., P. W. Comisky, J. S. Crane, and D. Zillmann. (1980). Relationship between college teachers' use of humor in the classroom and students' evaluations of their teachers. *Journal of Educational Psychology* 72 (4): 511–19.

Bryant, J., P. W. Comisky, and D. Zillmann. (1979). Teachers' humor in the college classroom. *Communication Education* 28:110–28.

Burford, C. T. (1985). The relationship of principals' sense of humor and job robustness to school environment. PhD diss., Pennsylvania State Univ.

Burlington Liars' Club. (Winter 2007). Retrieved 3/5/08 from www.burlington-liarsclub.com/.

Burns, J. M. (1979). *Leadership*. New York: Harper and Row.

Cann, A., K. Holdt, and L. G. Calhoun. (1999). The roles of humor and sense of humor in responses to stressors. *HUMOR: International Journal of Humor Research* 12:177–93.

Casper, R. (1999). Laughter and humor in the classroom: Effects on test performance. PhD diss., Mississippi State Univ.

Center for Social Media. (2007). Recut, reframe, recycle. Retrieved 4/10/09 from www.centerforsocialmedia.org/resources/publications/recut_reframe_ recycle/.

Center for Social Media. (2008). The Code of Best Practices in Fair Use for Media Literacy Education. Retrieved 4/10/09 from centerforsocialmedia. org/medialiteracy.

Cerciello, C. (2001). The effects of humor on anxiety and conflict resolution skills in emotionally disturbed students. PhD diss., Seton Hall Univ.

Chapman, A. J. (1974). An experimental study of socially facilitated humorous laughter. *Psychological Reports* 35:727–34.

Chapman, A .J., and H. C. Foot, eds. (1977). *It's a funny thing, humour.* Oxford: Pergamon Press.

———. (2004). *Humor and laughter: Theory, research, and applications.* New Brunswick, NJ: Transaction Publishers.

Chapman, A. J., and N. J. Gadfield. (1976). Is sexual humor sexist? *Journal of Communication* 26 (3): 141–53.

Cogan, R., D. Cogan, W. Waltz, and M. McCue. (1987). Effects of laughter and relaxation on discomfort thresholds. *Journal of Behavioral Medicine* 10:139–44.

Coleman, J. G., Jr. (1992). All seriousness aside: The laughing-learning connection. *International Journal of Instructional Media* 19 (3): 269–76.

Collinson, D. L. (1988). "Engineering humour": Masculinity, joking and conflict in shop-floor relations. *Organization Studies* 9 (2): 181–99.

———. (2002). Managing humour. *Journal of Management Studies* 39:269–88.

Conkell, C. S. (1993). The effects of humor on communicating fitness concepts to high school students. PhD diss., Florida State Univ.

Coser, R. L. (1959). Some social functions of laughter: A study of humor in a hospital setting. *Human Relations* 12:171–82.

Cousins, N. (1979). *Anatomy of an illness as perceived by the patient: Reflections on healing and regeneration.* New York: Bantam.

Crawford, C. B. (1994a). Theory and implications regarding the utilization of strategic humor by leaders. *Journal of Leadership & Organizational Studies* 1:53–68

———. (1994b). Strategic humor in leadership: Practical suggestions for appropriate use. Paper presented at the meeting of the Kansas Leadership Forum, Salina, KS.

Creguer, T. (1991). Dissertations of the weird and famous. *Research Update* 20. Ann Arbor, MI: University Microfiche International, 4–5.

Cross, M. J. (1989). Leadership perceptions: The role of humor. PhD diss., Univ. of Pittsburgh.

Dandridge, T. C., I. Mitroff, and W. F. Joyce. (1980). Organizational symbolism: A topic to expand organizational analysis. *Academy of Management Review* 5:77–82.

Davis, A., and B. H. Kleiner. (1989). The value of humour in effective leadership. *Leadership and Organizational Development Journal* 10:i–iii.

de Bono, E. (1970). *Lateral thinking: Creativity step by step.* New York: Harper and Row.

———. (1985). *De Bono's thinking course.* New York: Facts on File. Retrieved from members.optusnet.com.au/~charles57/Creative/Techniques/sixhats .htm.

Deal, T. E., and A. A. Kennedy. (1999). *The new corporate cultures.* Revitalizing the workplace after downsizing, mergers and reengineering (Business Essentials) London: Texere.

Derks, P., and J. Berkowitz. (1989). Some determinants of attitudes toward a joker. *HUMOR: International Journal of Humor Research* 2:385–96.

Devadoss, S., and J. Foltz. (1996). Evaluation of factors influencing class attendance and performance. *American Journal of Agricultural Economics* 78:499–507.

Dewey, J. (1916). *Democracy and education.* New York: Macmillan Company.

———. (1997). *Experience and education.* New York: Touchstone.

Dickmann, M. H., and N. Standford-Blair. (2002). *Connecting leadership to the brain.* Thousand Oaks, CA: Corwin Press.

Dickmeyer, S. (1993). Humor as an instructional practice: A longitudinal content analysis of humor use in the classroom. Paper presented at the annual meeting of the Eastern Communication Association, New Haven, CT.

Dodge, B., and A. Rossett. (1982). Heuristic for humor in instruction. *NSPI Journal* 5:11–14.

Dole, B. (2001). *Great presidential wit.* New York: Scribner.

Duay, D. L. (2007). In their own words: Older adults' perceptions of effective and ineffective learning experiences. PhD diss., Florida Atlantic Univ.

Duncan, W. J. (1982). Humor in management: Prospects for administrative practice and research. *Academy of Management Review* 7:136–42.

Duncan, W. J., and J. P. Feisal. (1989). No laughing matter: Patterns of humor in the workplace. *Organizational Dynamics* 17:18–30.

Duncan, W. J., L. R. Smeltzer, and T. L. Leap. (1990). Humor and work: Applications of joking behavior to management. *Journal of Management* 16 (2): 255–78.

Dwyer, T. (1991). Humor, power, and change in organizations. *Human relations* 44 (1): 1–13.

Edwards, C. M., and E. R. Gibboney. (1992). The power of humor in the college classroom. Paper presented at the annual meeting of the Western States Communication Association, Boise, ID.

Fadiman, C., ed. (1985). *The Little, Brown book of anecdotes*. Boston: Little, Brown & Co.

Fiegelson, S. (1998). *Energize your meetings with laughter*. Alexandria, VA: Association for Supervision and Curriculum Development.

Fink, E. I., and B. A. Walker. (1977). Humorous responses to embarrassment. *Psychological Reports* 40:475–85.

Forbes, R. E. N. (1997). Humor as a teaching strategy to decrease anger in the classroom of students who are emotionally handicapped or severely emotionally disturbed. PhD diss., Union Institute.

Fredericks, J., P. Blumenfeld, and A. Paris. (2004). School engagement: Potential of the concept. *Review of Educational Research* 74 (7): 59–109.

Freud, S. (1960). *Jokes and their relation to the unconscious*. Trans. J. Strachey. New York: W. W. Norton. (Orig. pub. 1905.)

Fry, W. F., and M. Allen. (2004). Humor as a creative experience: The development of a Hollywood humorist. In Chapman and Foot 2004, 245–58.

Fullen, M. (2001). *The new meaning of educational change*. 3rd ed. New York: Teachers College Press.

Gardner, H. (1996). *Leading minds: An anatomy of leadership*. New York: Basic Books.

Garner, R. L. (2006). Humor in pedagogy: How ha-ha can lead to aha! *College Teaching* 54 (1): 177–80.

Gates, W. I. E. Quote. *In The minimum daily adult: The right metrics and the wrong metrics*, by D. Kalm. Retrieved 2/13/09 from regions.cmg.org/regions/cacmg/THE%20MINIMUM%20DAILY%20ADULT%20-%20CA-CMG.pdf.

Gentile, L., and M. McMillan. (1987). *Stress and reading difficulties: Research, assessment, and intervention*. Newark, DE: International Reading Association.

Gesell, I. (1997). *Playing along: 37 group learning activities borrowed from improvisational theater*. Duluth, MN: Whole Person Associates.

Gibb, J. D. (1964). An experimental comparison of the humorous lecture and the nonhumorous lecture in informative speaking. Master's thesis, Univ. of Utah.

Giles, H., R. Y. Bourhis, N. J. Gadfield, G. J. Davies, and A. P. Davies. (1976). Cognitive aspects of humour in social interaction: A model and some linguistic data. In Chapman and Foot 2004, 139–54.

Glenn, R. (2002). Brain research: Practical applications for the classroom. *Teaching for Excellence* 21 (6): 1–2.

Glueck, I. (2001). Why do we laugh? A multidimensional theory. PhD diss., Saybrook Graduate School and Research Center.

Goldstein, J. H. (1976). Theoretical notes on humor. *Journal of Communication* 26 (3): 104–12.

Goleman, D. (1997). *Emotional intelligence: Why it can matter more than IQ.* New York: Bantam.

Gorham, J., and D. M. Christophel. (1990). The relationship of teachers' use of humor in the classroom to immediacy and student learning. *Communication Education* 39:46–62.

Graham, E. E., M. J. Papa, and G. P. Brooks. (1992). Functions of humor in conversation: Conceptualization and measurement. *Western Journal of Communication* 56 (2): 161–83.

Groening, M. (1986). *Work is hell.* New York: Pantheon.

Grugulis, I. (2002). Nothing serious? Candidates' use of humour in management training. *Human Relations* 55 (4): 387–406.

Gruner, C. R. (1965). An experimental study of satire as persuasion. *Speech Monographs* 32:149–54.

———. (1966). A further experimental study of satire as persuasion. *Speech Monographs* 33:184–85.

———. (1967a). An experimental study of editorial satire as persuasion. *Journalism Quarterly* 44:727–30.

———. (1967b). Effect of humor on speaker ethos and audience information gain. *Journal of Communication* 17:228–33.

———. (1971). An experimental study of ad hominem editorial satire: Art Hoppe vs. Martha Mitchell. Paper presented at the Speech Communication Association convention, San Francisco.

———. (1972). Self- and other-disparaging wit/humor and speaker ethos: Three experiments. ERIC Clearinghouse on Reading and Communication Skills.

———. (1978). *Understanding laughter: The workings of humor.* Chicago: Nelson-Hall.

———. (1985). Advice to the beginning speaker on using humor—what the research tells us. *Communication Education* 34:140–44.

Gunning, B. L. (2001). The role that humor plays in shaping organizational culture. PhD diss., Univ. of Toledo.

Gurtler, L. (2002). Humor in educational contexts. Paper presented at the annual meeting of the American Psychological Association, Chicago.

Guthrie, P. (1999). Knowledge through humor: An original approach for teaching developmental readers. Paper presented at the annual meeting of the National Institute for Staff and Organizational Development International Conference on Teaching and Leadership Excellence, Austin.

Hampes, W. P. (2001). Relation between humor and empathic concern. *Psychological Reports* 88:241–44.

Handey, J. (n.d.) *Deep thoughts*. Retrieved 3/5/08 from www.deepthoughtsby-jackhandey.com/.

Hauck, W. E., and J. W. Thomas. (1972). The relationship of humor to intelligence, creativity, and intentional and incidental learning. *Journal of Experimental Education* 40 (4): 52–55.

Haugen, T., and J. M. Melhus. (2006). *Latterling Lønnsomt!* Self-published.

Hebert, P. J. (1991). Humor in the classroom: Theories, functions, and guidelines. Paper presented at the annual meeting of the Central States Communication Association, Chicago.

Hill, D. J. (1988). *Humor in the classroom: A handbook for teachers (and other entertainers!)*. Springfield, IL: Charles C. Thomas.

Hodges, D. (2006). *Laugh lines for educators*. Thousand Oaks, CA: Corwin Press.

Hodgin, M. (1998). *1001 more humorous illustrations for public speaking: Fresh, timely, and compelling illustrations for preachers, teachers, and speakers*. Grand Rapids, MI: Zondervan.

Holmes, J. (2000). Politeness, power and provocation: How humour functions in the workplace. *Discourse Studies* 2 (2): 159–85.

Howard, P. J. (2002). *The owner's manual for the brain*. 2nd ed. Atlanta, GA: Bard Press.

Hudson, G. (1979). The role of humor in John F. Kennedy's 1960 presidential campaign. PhD diss., Southern Illinois Univ.

Hudson, K. (2001). Transforming a conservative company: One laugh at a time. *Harvard Business Review* (July–August): 45–53.

Hughes, P. (1983). *More on oxymoron*. New York: Penguin.

Humke, C., and C. E. Schaefer. (1996). Sense of humor and creativity. *Perceptual and Motor Skills* 82:544–47.

*HUMOR: International Journal of Humor Research*. L. E. Mintz, editor in chief. Mouton de Gruyter.

Humphreys, B. R. (1990). A cheerful heart is good medicine: The emotional and physical benefits of humor. Doctoral research paper, Biola Univ.

Hurren, B. L. (2001). The effects of principals' humor on teachers' job satisfaction. PhD diss., Univ. of Nevada, Reno.

InSight, Syncurde Canda Ltd., Communications Division. (1998). Retrieved 12/9/08 from home.comcast.net/~mr_ballard/Global%20%20Files/Strive%20For%20Perfection.pdf.

Jensen, E. (2008). A fresh look at brain-based education. *Phi Delta Kappan* 89 (6): 409–17.

Kahn, W. A. (1989). Toward a sense of organizational humour: Implications for organizational diagnosis and change. *Journal of Applied Behavioral Science* 25 (1): 45–64.

Kaplan, H. B., and I. H. Boyd. (1965). The social functions of humor on an open psychiatric ward. *Psychiatric Quarterly* 39:502–15.

Kets de Vries, M. F. R. (1990). The organizational fool: Balancing a leader's hubris. *Human Relations* 43 (8): 751–70.

Kher, N., S. Molstad, and R. Donahue. (1999). Using humor in the college classroom to enhance teaching effectiveness in "dread courses." *College Student Journal* 33 (3): 400–406.

King, J. (1999). Laughter and lesson plans. *Techniques* 74 (1): 34.

Klapp, O. E. (1949). The fool as a social type. *American Journal of Sociology* 55 (2): 157–62.

Klesius, J., K. Laframboise, and M. Gaier. (1998). Humorous literature: Motivation for reluctant readers. *Reading Research and Instruction* 37 (4): 253–61.

Koncz, J. R. (2001). Rhetorically analyzing humor: A methodology for studying humor as a rhetorical strategy. PhD diss., Arizona State Univ.

Koonce, W. J., III. (1997). The relationship between principals' humor styles and school climate in elementary schools (leadership, teachers). PhD diss., George Washington Univ.

Krisko, M. E. (2001). Teacher leadership: A profile to identify the potential. Paper presented at the biennial convocation of Kappa Delta Phi, Orlando.

Kuhrik, M. (1996). A comparison of humor using the situational humor response questionnaire and the coping humor scale by nontraditional and traditional students in midwestern schools of nursing. PhD diss., Southern Illinois Univ.

Kuiper, N., M. Grimshaw, C. Leite, and G. Kirsh. (2004). Humor is not always the best medicine: Specific components of sense of humor and psychological well-being. *Humor* 17 (1/2): 135–68.

LaCroix, D. (2001). *Learn how the pros make 'em laugh.* Audio learning program, 4 CD set.

La Fave, L., J. Haddad, and W. A. Maesen. (2004). Superiority, enhanced self-esteem, and perceived incongruity humor theory. In Chapman and Foot 2004, 63–92.

Leacock, S. (1937). *Humour and humanity: An introduction to the study of humour.* London: Thornton Butterworth.

Levine, J., ed. (2006). *Motivation in humor.* New Brunswick, NJ: Transaction Publishers.

Linstead, S. (1985). Jokers wild: The importance of humour in the maintenance of organizational culture. *Sociological Review* 33:741–67.

Lowman, J. (1994). Professors as performers and motivators. *College Teaching* 42 (4): 137–41.

Lundberg, C. C. (1969). Person-focused joking: Pattern and function. *Human Organization* 28:22–28.

Lyttle, J. (2001). The effectiveness of humor in persuasion: The case of business ethics training. PhD diss., York Univ.

Malone, P. B. (1980). Humor: A double-edged tool for today's managers? *Academy of Management Review* 5:357–60.

Malpass, L. F., and E. D. Fitzpatrick. (1959). Social facilitation as a factor in reaction to humor. *Journal of Social Psychology* 50:295–303.

Manning, K. (2002). Lighten up: An analysis of the role of humor as an instructional practice in the urban and/or culturally diverse middle school classroom. PhD diss., Cleveland State Univ.

Marken, D. J. (1999). An exploratory study of the ways principals use humor and perceive that humor contributes to their leadership. PhD diss., Univ. of La Verne.

Martin, D. M. (2001). Women, work, and humor: Negotiating paradoxes of organizational life. PhD diss., Univ. of Utah.

Martin, R. A., and J. P. Dobbin (1985). Sense of humor, hassles, and immunoglobulin A: Evidence for stress-moderating effect of humor. *International Journal of Psychiatry in Medicine* 18 (2): 93–105.

Martin, R. A., and H. M. Lefcourt. (1984). Situational Humor Response Questionnaire: Quantitative measure of sense of humor. *Journal of Personality and Social Psychology* 47 (1): 145–55.

Martineau, W. H. (1972). A model of the social functions of humor. In *The psychology of humor: Theoretical perspectives and empirical issues*, ed. J. H. Goldstein and P. E. McGhee, 101–25. New York: Academic.

Marzano, R. (2007). *The art and science of teaching: A comprehensive framework for effective instruction*. Alexandria, VA: Association for Supervision and Curriculum Development.

Masten, A. S. (1983). Humor and creative thinking in stress-resistant children. PhD diss., Univ. of Minnesota.

McGhee, P. E. (1976). Children's appreciation of humor: A test of the cognitive congruency principle. *Child Development* 47:420–26.

———. (1979). *Humor, its origin and development*. San Francisco: W. H. Freeman.

McGhee, P. E., and J. Goldstein, eds. (1983). *Handbook of humor research*. Vol. 2. New York: Springer-Verlag.

McKenzie, E. C. (1980). *14,000 quips and quotes for writers and speakers*. New York: Greenwich House.

McMorris, R. F., R. A. Boothroyd, and D. J. Pietrangelo. (1997). Humor in educational testing: A review and discussion. *Applied Measurement in Education* 10 (3): 269–97.

Metcalf, C. W., and R. Felible (1992). *Lighten up: Survival skills for people under pressure*. New York: Perseus Books.

Meyer, J. (1990). Ronald Reagan and humor: A politician's velvet weapon. *Communication Studies* 41 (1): 76–88.

Michaels, S. (1998). Cognitive and affective responses to humorous advertisements. PhD diss., Wayne State Univ.

Miner, F. C. (1979). A comparative analysis of three diverse group decision making approaches. *Academy of Management Journal* 22 (1): 81–93.

Mitchell, L. S. (2005). Learning through laughter: A study on the use of humor in interactive classrooms. PhD diss., Mississippi State Univ.

Moger, A. (1979). *The complete pun book*. Secaucus, NJ: Citadel.

Morreall, J. (1991). Humor and work. *HUMOR: International Journal of Humor Research* 4 (3/4): 359–74.

Munde, G. (1997). What are you laughing at? Differences in children's and adults' humorous book selections for children. *Children's Literature in Education* 28 (4): 219–33.

Nadeau, A., and M. S. Leighton. (1996). *The role of leadership in sustaining school reform: Voices from the field*. Washington, DC: U.S. Government Printing Office.

Neuendorf, K. A., and T. Fennel. (1988). A social facilitation view of the generation of humor and mirth reactions: Effects of a laugh track. *Central States Speech Journal* 39 (1): 37–48.

Novak, W., and M. Waldoks, eds. (1990). *The big book of new American humor: The best of the past 25 years*. New York: Harper Perennial.

O'Connell, W. E. (1960). The adaptive functions of wit and humor. *Journal of Abnormal and Social Psychology* 61:263–70.

Pedde, R. K. (1996). Laugh with me: Humor in the classroom. PhD diss., Pacific Lutheran Univ.

Perret, G. (1998). *Business humor: Jokes and how to deliver them*. New York: Sterling Publishing.

Philbrick, K. D. (1989). The use of humor and effective leadership styles. PhD diss., Univ. of Florida.

———. (1991). Put some levity into leadership. *Executive Educator* 13 (8): 27.

Phillips, K. A. (2000). The use of humor and effective leadership styles by elementary principals in Central Florida. PhD diss., Univ. of Central Florida.

Pierson, P., and P. Bredeson. (1993). It's not just a laughing matter: School principals' use of humor in interpersonal communications with teachers. *Journal of School Leadership* 3 (5): 522–33.

Pogrebin, M. R., and E. D. Poole. (1988). Humor in the briefing room: A study of the strategic uses of humor among police. *Journal of Contemporary Ethnography* 17:183–210.

Pollak, J. P., and P. D. Freda. (1997). Humor, learning, and socialization in middle level classrooms. *Clearing House* 70 (4): 176–78.

Pollio, H. R., and C. K. Bainum. (1983). Are funny groups good at solving problems? A methodological evaluation and some preliminary results. *Small Group Behavior* 14 (4): 379–404.

Pollio, H. R., and W. Humphreys. (1996). What award-wining lecturers say about their teaching: It's all about connection. *College Teaching* 44 (3): 101–6.

Poole, M. S. (1985). Tasks and interaction sequences: A theory of coherence in group decision-making interaction. In *Sequence and pattern in communicative behavior*, ed. R. L. Street, Jr., and J. N. Cappella, 206–24. Baltimore, MD: Edward Arnold.

Priest, R. F., and J. Swain. (2002). Humor and its implications for leadership effectiveness. *Humor* 15 (2): 169–89.

Prince, D., and M. Hoppe. (2000). *Communicating across cultures*. Greensboro, NC: Center for Creative Leadership.

Prosser, B. R., Jr. (1997). The use of humor among adult educators in formal classroom settings. PhD diss., North Carolina State Univ.

Provine, R. (2000). *Laughter: A scientific investigation*. New York: Penguin.

Putnam, R. (2000). *Bowling alone*. New York: Simon & Schuster.

Ramirez, C. M. (2002). What is the impact of humor, message content and the leader's gender on perceptions of credibility of a leader? PhD diss., Our Lady of the Lake Univ.

Rareshide, S. W. (1993). Implications for teachers' use of humor in the classroom. Retrieved from the ERIC Document Reproduction Service No. ED 359 165

Reynolds, K. C., and C. E. Nunn. (1997). Engaging classrooms: Student participation and the instructional factors that shape it. Paper presented at the annual meeting of the Association for the Study of Higher Education.

Ritter, D. P. (1997). Humor as a teaching methodology: The Tamashiro and Bandes model, its impact upon first grade student achievement in the language arts. PhD diss., Univ. of Bridgeport.

Romer, D. (1993). Do students go to class? Should they? *Journal of Economic Perspectives* 7 (3): 167–74.

Rose, E. (n.d.). *Southwest Airlines jokes*. Retrieved 11/22/07 from gosw.about.com/od/resortsandtours/a/swjokes.htm.

Ruth, C. (1999). Laughter and humor in the classroom. PhD diss., Univ. of Nebraska.

Salkind, N. J. (2000). *Statistics for people who (think they) hate statistics*. Thousand Oaks, CA: Sage Publications.

Schill, T., and S. O'Laughlin. (1984). Humor preference and coping with stress. *Psychological Reports* 55:309–10.

Schmidt, S. R., and A. R. Williams. (2001). Memory and humorous cartoons. *Memory and Cognition* 29 (2): 305–11.

Scogin, F. R., Jr., and H. R. Pollio. (1980). Targeting and the humorous episode in group process. *Human Relations* 33:831–52.

Scriven, J., and L. Hefferin. (1998). Humor: The "witting" edge in business. *Business Education Forum* 52 (3): 13–15.

Seuss, Dr. [Theodor Seuss Geisel]. (1957). *The cat in the hat*. New York: Random House.

Shade, R. A. (1996). *License to laugh: Humor in the classroom*. Westport, CT: Teacher Ideas Press.

Sheppard, L. M. (2002). The effect of humor in instructional text on learning, interest, and enjoyment: Is good humor just for ice cream? PhD diss., Michigan State University.

Simons, G. (1997). The uses and abuses of humor in a multicultural world. *Managing Diversity* (October): 1–3.

Sleeter, M. (1981). Are you "humoring" your employees? *Management World* 10:25–27.

Smidl, S. L. (2006). Portraits of laughter in "kid"ergarten children: The giggles and guffaws that support teaching, learning, and relationships. PhD diss., Virginia Polytechnic Institute and State Univ.

Smith, C. M., and L. Powell. (1988). The use of disparaging humor by group leaders. *Southern Speech Communication Journal* 53 (3): 279–92.

Smith, E. E., and H. L. White. (1965). Wit, creativity, and sarcasm. *Journal of Applied Psychology* 49:131–34.

Sousa, D. (1995). *How the brain learns: A classroom teacher's guide*. Reston, VA: National Association of Secondary Schools Principals.

Stanford-Blair, N., and M. Dickmann. (2005). *Leading coherently: Reflections from leaders around the world*. Thousand Oaks, CA: Sage Publications.

Sternberg, R. J., ed. (1990). *Handbook of human intelligence*. 2nd ed. New York: Cambridge University Press.

Stephenson, R. M. (1951). Conflict and control functions of humor. *American Journal of Sociology* 56:569–74.

Stephenson, S., and P. Thibault. (2006). *Laughing matters: Strategies for building a joyful learning community*. Bloomington, IN: Solution Tree.

Stevenson, D. (2005). *Signature Stories*. Retrieved 4/14/08 from www.bradmontgomery.com/general/signature-stories-2/.

St. Pierre, J. (2001). Student evaluation of a teacher's use of student-disparaging versus self-disparaging humor. PhD diss., Univ. of Alabama.

Stuart, W., and L. Rosenfeld. (June 1994). Student perceptions of teacher humor and classroom climate. *Communication Research Reports* 11 (1): 87–97.

Swanson, D. J. (1996). Humor as presentational device in broadcast public service announcements. Paper presented at the Southwest Symposium of the Southwest Council for Journalism and Mass Communication, Monroe, LA.

Swift, W. B., and A. T. Swift. (1994). Humor experts jazz up the workplace. *HR Magazine on Human Resources* 39 (3): 72–75.

Taft, R. A. (n.d.). Humorous quotes about statistics. Retrieved 4/13/09 from www.workinghumor.com/quotes/statistics.shtml.

Talbot, L. A. (1996). The association between sense of humor, coping ability and burnout among nursing education faculty. PhD diss., Univ. of North Texas.

Teslow, J. L. (1995a). An evaluation of humor as a motivational, cognitive, and affective enhancement to learn feedback and remediation strategies in computer-based instruction. PhD diss., Univ. of Colorado, Denver.

———. (1995b). Humor me: A call for research. *Educational Technology Research & Development* 43 (3): 6–28.

Thomas, S. E. (2001). An investigation into the use of humor for coping with stress. PhD diss., Univ. of Waterloo, Canada.

Thompson, J. L. (2000). Funny you should ask, what is the effect of humor on memory and metamemory? PhD diss., American Univ.

Torok, S. E., R. F. McMorris, and Lin Wen-Chi. (2004). Is humor an appreciated teaching tool? *College Teaching* 52 (1): 14–20.

Townsend, M. A., et al. (1983). Student perceptions of verbal and cartoon humor in the test situation. *Educational Research Quarterly* 7 (4): 17–23.

Tribble, M. K., Jr. (2001). Humor and mental effort in learning. PhD diss., Univ. of Georgia.

Tumkaya, S. (2007). Burnout and humor relationship among university lecturers. *HUMOR: International Journal of Humor Research* 20 (1): 73–92.

Tuttle, A. C. (2006). Humor and leadership: Subordinate perceptions of principal effectiveness as influenced by humor. PhD diss., Central Michigan Univ.

University of Maryland. (2000). Laughter is good for your heart, according to a new University of Maryland Medical Center study. American Heart Association's Scientific Sessions 2000, New Orleans. Retrieved 4/15/09 from www.umm.edu/news/releases/laughter.htm.

Vega, G. M. (1990). Humor competence: The fifth component. Paper presented at the annual meeting of the Teachers of English to Speakers of Other Languages, San Francisco.

Vinton, K. L. (1989). Humor in the workplace: It is more than telling jokes. *Small Group Behavior* 20 (2): 151–66.

Vogel, M. R. (1995). Is humor a useful teaching tool in human sexuality education? Perspectives of sixth-grade students. PhD diss., Univ. of Pennsylvania.

Von Oech, R. (1990). *A whack on the side of the head: How you can be more creative.* Rev. ed. New York: Warner Books.

Wallinger, L. M. (1997). Don't smile before Christmas: The role of humor in education. *NASSP Bulletin* 81 (589): 27–34.

Walters, L. (1995). *What to say when . . . you're dying on the platform.* New York: McGraw-Hill.

Wanzer, M. B., A. Frymier, A. Wojtaszczyk, and T. Smith. (2006). Appropriate and inappropriate uses of humor by teachers. *Communication Education* 55 (2): 178–96.

Wanzer, M. B., et al. (1995). Are funny people popular? An examination of humor orientation, loneliness, and social attraction. *Communication Quarterly* 44 (Winter): 42–52.

Weinstein, M., speaker. (1986). *Lighten up: The power of humor at work.* Audio recording. Greenwich, CT: Listen USA.

Weise, R. E. (1996). Quality of life and sense of humor in college students. PhD diss., Univ. of Maryland, College Park.

Welford, T. W. (1971). An experimental study of the effectiveness of humor used as a refutational device. PhD diss., Louisiana State Univ. and Agricultural & Mechanical College.

Westcott, R. S. (1983). Self-generated humor as an alternative in identifying potentially gifted, talented and creative high school students: An exploratory study. PhD diss., Univ. of Georgia.

Westwood, R. (2004). Comic relief: Subversion and catharsis in organizational comedic theatre. *Organization Studies* 25 (5): 775–95.

White, E. B. Quotation details. Retrieved 4/1/09 from www.quotationspage.com/quote/984.html.

White, F. (1992). Enhancing class attendance. *National Association of Colleges and Teachers in Agriculture Journal* 36:113–15.

Wierzbicki, M., and R. Young. (1978). The relation of intelligence and task difficulty to appreciation of humor. *Journal of General Psychology* 99 (1): 25–32.

Wilkins, J. (2006). An examination of the student and teacher behaviors that contribute to good student-teacher relationships in large urban high schools. PhD diss., State Univ. of New York, Buffalo.

Williams, C. F. (2001). Humor and the retention of lecture material by student-athletes in a mentor information session. PhD diss., Pennsylvania State Univ.

Williams, R. A., and R. W. Clouse. (1991). *Humor as a management technique: Its impact on school culture and climate.*

Willard, M. (2006). Humor in the hands of seasoned montessorians. *Montessori Life: A Publication of the American Montessori Society* 18 (2): 50–53.

Wilson, V. (April, 1999). Student response to a systematic program of anxiety-reducing strategies in a graduate-level introductory educational research course. Paper presented at the annual meeting of the Association of Educational Research Association.

Winnick, C. (1976). The social contexts of humor. *Journal of Communication* 26 (3): 124–28.

Wolfe, P. (2001). *Brain matters: Translating research into classroom practice.* Alexandria, VA: Association for Supervision and Curriculum Development.

Wooten, P. (1996). Humor: An antidote for stress. *Holistic Nursing Practice* 10 (2): 49–55.

Young, B. N., M. E. Whitley, and C. Helton. (1998). Students' perceptions of characteristics of effective teachers. Paper presented at the annual meeting of the Mid-South Educational Research Association, New Orleans.

Young, J. Short and sweet: Technology shrinks the lecture. Retrieved 4/14/09 from chronicle.com/free/v54/i41/41a00901.htm.

Zemke, R. (1991). Humor in training: Laugh and the world learns with you—maybe. *Training* 28 (8): 26–29.

Ziegler, V., G. Boardman, and M. D. Thomas. (1985). Humor, leadership, and school climate. *Clearing House* 58 (8):346–48.

Zillmann, D., and S. H. Stocking. (1976). Putdown humor. *Journal of Communication* 26 (3): 154–63.

Ziv, A. (1984). *Personality and sense of humor.* New York: Springer.

———. (1988). Teaching and learning with humor: Experiment and replication. *Journal of Experimental Education* 57 (1): 5–15.

# ABOUT THE AUTHOR

**Peter M. Jonas** is chair of the Doctoral Leadership Studies Department and professor at Cardinal Stritch University, teaching graduate-level courses in research, history, and leadership. He has served as a college professor, educational consultant, speaker, and author for more than thirty years, becoming well known for his sense of humor and lectures on humor.